IF YOU DON'T DO POLITICS, POLITICS WILL DO YOU...

Endorsements

"Politics is prevalent in all organisations. I have yet to find an organisation, large or small, that is devoid of political wrangling. You can try to ignore it, yet it will slowly but surely frustrate and distract you and inevitably derail your career. Or you can strive to understand it to be proactive in dealing with it in productive ways. If you want to understand organisational politics, this is an excellent guide. It is full of practical insight, useful frameworks, and relevant tools. This short, sharp, and valuable book will give you the perspective you need to understand and navigate the myriad of complex relationships you will invariably confront in any organisation; it will change your perspective and empower you to be way more productive in an organisational setting."

Dr Greg Fisher, Editor In Chief, "Business Horizons," Professor of Entrepreneurship at Kelley School of Business, Indiana, United States

"This is a very practical and well written guide on all things office politics! What we typically refer to as 'politics' is properly termed 'bad politics', given the connotations of negative, insidious, self-serving and destructive behaviors with the book providing useful suggestions on how one can navigate that terrain. Interestingly, the book also develops the notion of 'good politics' and how we should leverage that for good and to further any organisation's objectives. It also has plenty (and, sometimes, funny!) anecdotes that are totally relatable. Learn how to distinguish the politics and respond accordingly – to defuse or amplify. This is a recommended and empowering read for anyone working with people!"

Dr. Jackie Chimhanzi, CEO African Leadership Institute

"Niven has masterfully captured the essence of organisational politics, and how to manage it successfully – with dignity and poise. This is a must-read for any leader – understanding and perfecting these unspoken "rules of the game" will help you navigate the cross-currents that occur when working within any organisational structure. Thank you, Niven, for distilling many years of experience, failures and successes and turning them into a practical guide."

Deon Greyling, Senior Vice President, BTS Middle East

"If you are a leader who is of the opinion that you don't do politics, then this book is a must read. It poses strong challenges and quiet invitations at the same time. Challenges to understand the playing field of modern business and ourselves and others in that arena. Exciting invitations of how to play the best game, to be a source of positive energy and influence others in order to achieve amazing business and personal results. Niven has combined the rigour of researching practical, easy to apply models with the vulnerability of personal anecdotes in an easy to read, very useful guide to achieving success as a leader in and out of the executive suite."

Desray Shuck, Head: Leadership Development, Anglo American

"This book is an eye-opener. Niven puts her finger on the core issues around office politics and decodes the opaque with ruthless intelligence and clarity. Her insights are based on management research as well as broad and deep personal experience in different types of organisations. She brings out the necessary and positive as well as the potentially toxic and avoidable aspects of office politics in a manner that makes sense and holds concrete lessons for application in the world today. I warmly recommend this book."

Rebekka Grun von Jolk, Team Leader:
Human Development Africa, World Bank

"We hear of corporate politics every day, even though we hate the mention of the word. Yet our lives are surrounded by politics, very few of us know how to authentically navigate through office politics effectively and ethically, not knowing what to do about it. Niven Postma speaks simply, genuinely and yet cleverly on the topic. As a corporate professional who prides himself on the value of hard work and meritocracy I badly needed to hear Niven's practical insights and wisdom to win through the corporate landscape. I read this book during lockdown at my home in Johannesburg, South Africa and felt as though I was in a front row seat in her lecture or workshop having an experience on how I can be greater at work by making small changes for big results. It's a definitive guide to working politically smarter!"

Ben Matai, Vice-President, HR and Corporate Affairs, Sasol Mining

"This wonderful piece of work focuses necessary attention on the frequently misunderstood world of office politics. Niven lends her vast life and work experience to this crucial topic, and with vulnerability and transparency explores the rather murky world we navigate as individuals and groups in organisations. The relevant models and theories cited enable the reader to create meaning in their own context. These, in addition to the real-life scenarios, create hooks from which to hang new learnings and stimulate new ways of thinking and being in our own workplaces and communities. Thanks for an informative, practical and well-written guide."

Linda Buckley, Director: Executive Education,
Henley Business School, South Africa

"One of the messages I get from this very apt and entertaining book, is "Think twice, speak once, not the other way around". Another way of putting it, is whether at home or at work, observing and reflecting carefully is important and then clearly verbalising your thoughts equally so. No one can be expected to read your thoughts. Furthermore, often it is not what you say, but how you say it, and to whom, in which particular circumstances. I would love names to be attached to some of Niven's experiences. Would make for fascinating reading! This is recommended reading for all."

Russell Loubser, Retired CEO of the JSE, Director of Companies

"Empowering, enlightening and relevant. At a point in our lives we all experience the impact of what we see as inexplicable behaviours and decisions made in the name of what is vaguely explained away as 'politics'. Especially in our work lives. Niven has in her signature talk style, cut to the heart of this mysterious matter. She has made the unspoken spoken. Laid the hidden and concealed quite bare. That elusive and ghost-like character that has haunted the hallways of our corporate dead ends and befuddling project failures has been unmasked, named, deconstructed and now stands clearly illumined for anyone willing to conquer. The reader will feel inducted into the powerful and secret societies they always suspected existed but could just never get into. Anyone trying to achieve big goals and success in an organisational setting stands to benefit from this read. The career trajectory that many still long for but had seemed more and more unlikely is suddenly a possibility again by applying the concrete approaches shared in this book. I personally felt enlightened, empowered and in some cases even vindicated by the stories and insights on politics and their potential impacts at work."

Lolly Gwabavu, Coach and Leadership Development Specialist

"I attended Niven's workshop when I was reeling from a career disaster. That one day gave me valuable insights into what had caused the disaster, my role in the disaster, and the changes I needed to make to safeguard myself going forward. The 'aha' moments I had that day are all contained in these valuable pages. Reading them now, I'm so grateful for Niven's wisdom and guidance. And I'm so proud of the progress I've made since then. Read this book!"

Jenefer Morgan (CA)SA, MBA, Head: People,
Boost & Co, United Kingdom

"For many professionals, networking and office politics are "Four Letter Words" – hissed under one's breath. Worse, insecurity and resentment around these topics means capable people miss out on opportunities for which they're well positioned. Niven brings her breadth of experience – multi-discipline, multi-national, multi-cultural – to offer an integrated approach to office politics. She demystifies the "why" and the "how" so professionals can have more influence, get more done and experience more satisfaction at work – and arguably outside work, too. Reading this book was like the best seminar with Niven – fun, thought-provoking and highly action-oriented. I highly recommend it."

Greg Durst, Managing Director, Corporate Development & Events,
Institutional Limited Partners Association, Canada

"Well done for tackling such a charged topic with humour and personal anecdotes. Sharing your successes as well as your failures is a brave thing to do, but this is exactly what makes this such a valuable and practical guide on how to navigate the complex and often opaque world or corporate power and politics. Interwoven with the more academic references and practical self-assessment exercises, you tell a great story in an accessible and easy-to-read way."

Marina Bidoli, Partner and Office Head: Brunswick, South Africa

"Niven's book is at once an academic primer on human social psychology and a memoir from the school of hard knocks. She has, with a few words, models, and stories managed to distil down the real-world challenges of navigating office politics and has offered an approachable guide to successfully achieving both personal and corporate ambitions ethically. I appreciate books that don't just describe the theory, but give you practical self-tests and exercises to implement their wisdom – this one does that."

Christopher Malan, Managing Director,
ELB Equipment, Sydney, Australia

"Realising your working purpose is impossible without understanding and working the politics, as Niven reflects so clearly. This book resonates with those typical frustrations of complex modern working life and offers practical, humorous ways to wise up and get ahead personally whilst focusing on getting the right job done. It's a treat and easy to read."

Robert Urry, Director – Banking Supervision Special Teams,
Central Bank of the UAE

"It is commonly thought that you can either play the political game or be a decent person, but not both. But is that true? Drawing on the best research and her own diverse experience, Niven Postma will help you to understand why workplace politics are inevitable and how you can navigate office politics in order to be both useful and successful. Read this if you stick your nose up at politics but feel frustrated as you watch others use politics to their benefit."

Liz Wiseman, New York Times bestselling author of Multipliers and Rookie Smarts

First published in 2020.

ISBN: 978-1-86922-852-1
eISBN: 978-1-86922-853-8

Published by KR Publishing
P O Box 3954
Randburg
2125

Republic of South Africa

Tel: (011) 706-6009
Fax: (011) 706-1127
E-mail: orders@knowres.co.za
Website: www.kr.co.za

Typesetting, layout and design: Cia Joubert, cia@knowres.co.za
Cover design: Marlene De Lorme, marlene@knowres.co.za
Proofreading: Valda Strauss: valda@global.co.za
Project management: Cia Joubert, cia@knowres.co.za

DON'T DO POLITICS, POLITICS WILL DO YOU...

A guide to navigating office politics
effectively and ethically
[And yes, it is possible]

NIVEN POSTMA

publishing

2020

Acknowledgements

Helen Nicholson, the wonderful and wise friend who started me on this path in the first place. How true it is, Helly, that "the obstacle is the way".

All the delegates who attend my lectures and workshops. Your stories, insights and experiences enrich me every time I get to share mine with you.

Yvette Nowell, the best supporter and partner I could possibly have wished for. My world and the world are made infinitely better by having you in it.

Table of Contents

About the author

Niven Postma has had a wide and varied career across multiple organisations and sectors, in South Africa and internationally, including being first CEO of the Businesswomen's Assocation (BWA), CEO of NOAH (Nurturing Orphans of AIDS for Humanity), Head of External Strategy and then Head of the SARB Academy at the South African Reserve Bank, and Head of Leadership and Culture for the Standard Bank Group. She is the MD of Niven Postma Inc. and works as a leadership, culture and strategy facilitator for clients around the world, including Australia, Germany, South Africa, the United Kingdom and the UAE. She holds a BA, EMBA and PG Dip in Futures Studies, is married and lives in Johannesburg, South Africa.

Introduction

Whenever I give a lecture or workshop on navigating office politics, I generally start by asking a few opening questions to get a feel for the delegates and the mood in the room. They are usually along the lines of:

"How many of you just *love* the idea of office politics?"

"How many of you think that work would be so much easier if it weren't for politics?"

And my favourite: "How many of you think that you just go to the office to do your job and put in a good day's work, and that it's everyone else who is playing politics?"

As you can imagine, very few hands usually go up in answer to the first two questions, while inevitably a *lot* (if not all) are raised in response to the last one. These opening minutes set the scene very effectively for a day of ideas, insights and stories that leave delegates understanding the nature and possibilities of organisational politics very differently. A day that also often leaves them – and me – profoundly moved.

Some of the responses at the end of a session include:

"I have spent 27 years in financial services, and this is the first time I've actually understood what is going on around me."

"If I had known just some of this stuff when I started working, I think my career could have been very different."

"Why does nobody teach us this stuff?"

"I think you may have just saved my job…"

Every time I get feedback like this, I realise, yet again, that despite politics being an inevitable part of every single organisation, most people are completely clueless when it comes to understanding office politics and knowing what to do about them. And they are *especially* clueless about the possibility of navigating politics ethically and in line with their values, for the benefit of themselves, their team and their organisation. Instead, the almost universally held view is that you can either play the political game, *or* you can be a decent person. You certainly cannot do, or be, both.

And so it's hardly surprising that people answer my questions in the ways that they do. With this kind of understanding of politics, who would want to own up to being part of something that we see as unpleasant at best and downright sordid at worst? Who would *not* want to stick their heads in the sand at work, hoping that the politics go away or, at the very least, not affect them too much?

This was precisely my view too, until I started researching the topic of organisational politics. This gave me the chance to better understand something which I had also made every effort to avoid in my career. It also allowed me to reflect deeply on my career. A career which has been very successful and resulted in many achievements that I am very proud of and one in which I have also made all kinds of naïve, stupid and avoidable political mistakes.

I spent two months putting together a day-long lecture that I hoped would be meaningful and paradigm-shifting, but also practical. The question I asked myself in deciding what to include and what to leave out was simple: "If I had known this during those times in my career when I was really struggling or unhappy and hitting my head against a brick wall, would it have made a difference?"

If the answer was "yes", I included the material. If the answer was "no", I filed it under "very interesting, but so what?" and left it out.

After two years of delivering the lecture as a core module in various leadership development programmes, it became very clear that what would have helped *me* would undoubtedly have helped other people too. This is what prompted me to write this book. It was an opportunity to get the word out to far more people than I will ever have the chance to meet in person, about how they can – and should – develop what is a critical set of skills for their career and personal success.

It really is true: "If you don't do politics, politics will do you."

CHAPTER 1

What Do We Mean by Office Politics?

*"Man's mind, once stretched by a new idea,
never regains its original dimensions."*

–Oliver Wendell Holmes

Given that so many of us are allergic to the concept of office politics, you would think that we would be clear on what they are. But in my experience, the vast majority of us have it completely wrong. Typically, when I ask people what office politics are, they volunteer things along the lines of:

> "It's a game that people play – one that doesn't feel fair because there are winners and losers, and some people know the rules and others don't."

> "It's about backstabbing and using others."

> "It's about climbing your way to the top, no matter what it takes."

Sound familiar? And yet, these definitions – all of them negative and unpleasant – are actually wrong. The correct definitions are actually much clearer and completely neutral, i.e. neither negative nor positive, pleasant nor unpleasant.

Here are a few that I particularly like:

"Organisational politics refers to a variety of activities associated with the use of influence tactics to improve personal or organisational interests."[1]

"Organisational politics are informal, unofficial, and sometimes behind-the-scenes efforts to sell ideas, influence an organisation, increase power, or achieve other targeted objectives."[2]

"Office politics can be understood as the unwritten rules that determine who gets what, when and how – a promotion, a budget for a project, a say in the boss's decisions – and who doesn't."[3]

To put it even more straightforwardly:

"Office politics is really just the art of influencing others so that we can get stuff done at work."[4]

Perhaps, when reading these, you are having the same reaction as many people – if these are the correct definitions, then it is less about *what* politics are and more about *how* people engage in them and *why*. *That's* what we don't like, what we find unfair and what we avoid being part of. And no doubt you have the same concerns, complaints and criticisms that I have heard repeatedly – stories of people being bullied, victimised, sidelined and all manner of other destructive and damaging things. Add to this, the implication that our careers depend on unwritten rules which are often very different to the official ones on paper, and it's not surprising that everything to do with politics can be interpreted as unfair, hypocritical and arbitrary, with those "on the inside" knowing the rules and benefiting from them and those "on the outside" just having to guess at them.

---

1   Jarrett, 2017.

2   Bauer & Erdogan, 2010.

3   Kaiser, Chamorro-Premuzic & Lusk, 2017.

4   McKee, 2015.

My response is that all of these things are true.

They are also, almost certainly, unavoidable.

We would be naïve to think otherwise. Power and the reality of organisational dynamics can bring out some truly toxic behaviour in people.

One of the most awful stories I heard in one of my lectures was from a woman who was probably in her early 30s. She told us of her very first day in her very first job at a company that every single person reading this book would know. She was bright-eyed and bushy-tailed and straight out of university. One of the first people in her family to have a degree and an office job, she was raring to get going and start what she hoped would be a brilliant career of doing amazing things in the world. Five minutes into meeting the first manager she had ever had, the words of wisdom and advice he chose to give her in her introduction to the organisation and the world of work were: "In this place, you either pull up your socks, or you pull down your pants…"

When I tell this story, people gasp and look utterly horrified, which is about right because it's an appalling thing to hear. However, this kind of example is still only one kind of story because power and organisations can also – and *should* also – bring out the best in people. One of the most profound TED talks I have ever watched was recorded in July 2009 by Chimamanda Adichie, the excellent Nigerian novelist.[5]

As of 25 March 2020, it has been watched 21 420 756 times (at least 42 of which were me) and is one of the top 10 TED talks of all time. I think there are many reasons for its popularity. For me, it was the power and insight of the concept that Ngozie Adichie introduces in the talk, namely "The Danger of the Single Story"; a concept which she then very eloquently elaborates on for 18 minutes and 34 seconds of wisdom and humour. As she puts it so perfectly at one point in the talk: "The single story creates stereotypes and the problem with stereotypes is not that they are untrue, but that they are incomplete. They make one story become the *only* story."

---

5   Ngozi Adichie, 2009.

I am always left humbled when I come face to face with my own single stories and realise (yet again) the limitations of my thinking and awareness. One of the most powerful examples of this for me was in the early 2000s when I was CEO of NOAH (Nurturing Orphans of AIDS for Humanity), during a time when the HIV-AIDS crisis was reaching desperate proportions in South Africa. NOAH was one of the largest NGOs for Orphaned and Vulnerable Children (OVC) in South Africa at the time, providing a range of care and support through community-run projects called Arks, to children and their caregivers. We had approximately 100 projects in peri-urban or rural areas across Gauteng and KwaZulu-Natal, caring for thousands of children every weekday.

One of our Arks was in Vosloorus, a township[6] on the East Rand of Johannesburg. One Friday, after spending most of the day there, I was tired and eager to get home. It had been a long week and I just wanted to have a hot bath and welcome the weekend. Being winter, it was starting to get dark relatively early. I had left later than normal, and somehow managed to get lost on my way from the Ark to the highway – a distance of no more than three or four kilometres and a route that I knew well.

Anyone who knows South African townships will know how haphazard the roads and signage can be, but I tried a few more turns before realising that I was well and truly lost. Since this was well before the days of GPS, I just kept going around in circles, hoping that sooner or later I would come

---

6   Apartheid was the system of institutionalised racial segregation that existed in South Africa and South West Africa (Namibia) from 1948 until the early 1990s. In terms of The Population Registration Act, every citizen of the country was classified by their race. The Group Areas Act was passed in 1950 and specified which areas of urban spaces could be occupied by which races. The key premise – as with all the elements of apartheid – was to keep the races separate. "Townships" commonly refers to those areas that were designated as living areas for black people. White suburbs were generally well laid out and maintained and situated close to employment opportunities and centres of business. Townships, by contrast, had far less infrastructure and resources. Since the repeal of Apartheid in 1991 many black, coloured and Indian people have settled in previously white suburbs. However the reverse has not happened to any great degree. As such while it is an everyday occurrrence to see people of all races mingling or living in previously white areas, including malls, workplaces and entertainment venues, it is still much less usual to see white people in townships. Consequently, it is not uncommon that I enter a township as a white person and have children staring, pointing and calling me 'umlungu' (white person).

across a street or a landmark that I recognised and be able to find my way to the N3 from there. That didn't happen.

Instead, just as I was coming around yet another corner, I saw a collection of taxis congregated on an open patch of ground. It wasn't a formal taxi rank; just a group of men standing around their taxis and talking. Seeing them, I was suddenly much happier, reasoning that of course if anyone would be able to direct me, it would be them.

I drove up to the very animated men, wound down my passenger window (yes, it was also before I had a car with electric windows) and explained my situation. Once they had recovered from their surprise at seeing a white woman in the township on a Friday night, they began sharing their road knowledge enthusiastically, explaining to me where I should go.

Clearly, I was looking as confused as I felt, because in the next second, one of the men leaned through my open passenger window, opened the door from the inside, plonked himself on my passenger seat, looked at me very confidently and told me firmly to "Just drive. I'll direct you and take you to where you need to go."

To say that I was nervous and uncomfortable is putting it, um, mildly. I had a complete stranger in my car, in the dark, with no idea of where I was or where he was taking me. All I could do was gulp and accept that I had no choice but to trust this man and the situation I was in, because there was no way to get out of it.

Of course, as is the case more often than not, things turned out perfectly well. In less than two minutes, my passenger had helped me back to the main road that I knew well and from where I could easily find my way back to the highway. I was tremendously relieved and grateful. I thanked him profusely for his kindness. He assured me that he knew a shortcut and so would get back to his taxi quickly and easily. With that, he jumped out of my car, leaned in my window and asked one last time if I would be okay.

"Absolutely! Thank you again."

"Are you sure? You know where you are, and you know how to get home from here?"

"100%! I'll be totally fine and home in 30 minutes, tops."

"Good! Well then, drive safely and get home safely, okay?"

"Definitely! Thank you again. I am so grateful for your help.

Goodbye!"

Just as he was about to leave, he decided to offer me one last, very stern piece of advice: "Go well and for *heaven's* sake, don't let just anyone in your car again, you hear?! It's not *safe*, my dear!"

I could only laugh and delight at this. I remember it often when I am tempted to lose my temper in traffic, as taxi drivers pull their crazy stunts on the roads of South Africa because, yes, it is absolutely true that they can be a real menace on the roads. But it is also not the whole story. We have 250,000 minibus taxis currently doing business in South Africa. The 15 million daily commuter trips that they undertake represent 75% of all transport to work, schools and universities in the country.[7] The competition is fierce and sometimes violent and the margins are thin and scarce.

It should be obvious that anything complex will always have more than a single story. But all too often we fall into the trap of the one dimensional, because it doesn't even occur to us to look for more. Exactly the same is true when it comes to the subject of office politics. There is so much more to office politics than the single negative and destructive story that we hear, tell ourselves and tell each other. This single story is damaging in the extreme, with all kinds of "opportunity costs, because it's a story of bad politics *only*."[8]

---

7   Wasserman, 2019.

8   Kaiser, Chamorro-Premuzic & Lusk, 2017.

"Bad politics are about the wrangling, manoeuvring, sucking up, backstabbing, and rumour mongering people use to advance themselves at the expense of other people or the organisation. Bad politics are, at their core, about promoting oneself by any means necessary. And really bad politics are about being sneaky, perhaps even Machiavellian or immoral, to intentionally harm someone else for personal gain."9

There is another story that very seldom gets talked about, if at all. And that's the story of good and necessary politics, which are also about going outside the usual, "formally sanctioned channels"10 to get things done, but in such a way that you advance your own interests as well as benefit whatever organisation you are in.11

9   Kaiser, Chamorro-Premuzic & Lusk, 2017.

10   Reardon, 2015.

11   Kaiser, Chamorro-Premuzic & Lusk, 2017.

Good politics are
about the completely
acceptable and
legitimate ways of
being recognised,
of influencing what
happens and doesn't, of
guiding what decisions
are made and not made
etc.

Bizarrely, but unsurprisingly given the predominance of the single negative story of politics, when people do these things, we don't see their actions as politics. Instead, we see it as them being 'savvy, well-networked, or street smart, socialising ideas, and managing stakeholders.'[12]

Of course, it's all of those things, but it is also politics. The bigger, more complete story of politics and how important *good* politics are, is a story that I invite you to start to rewrite in your own career as you read this book. This story will include a few of my own, personal examples – those where I've done well, but even more importantly, those where I have failed.

---

12 Kaiser, Chamorro-Premuzic & Lusk, 2017.

CHAPTER 2

So Do You Want The Good News or The Bad News?

"Without ambition one starts nothing. Without work one finishes nothing. The prize will not be sent to you. You have to win it."

–Ralph Waldo Emerson

"The question is not whether organisations will have politics, but what kind of politics they will have. Politics can be energising or debilitating, hostile or constructive, devastating or creative."[13]

In my experience, this is absolutely true, and it makes some people feel a lot better… and others a lot worse. On the one hand, understanding this inescapable fact of organisational life helps some people realise that they are not in a uniquely politicised environment and to accept that what they are experiencing is normal. The choice is then theirs as to what they want to do about it, but at least they are no longer under any illusions of their reality.

For others, it can be very difficult to accept that there is no magical place where politics don't exist and that if they "just keep trying", they will one day find it and work there. The truth is, there simply is no such place.

That is not just my opinion after having worked in all manner of contexts – from urban boardrooms to rural communities, in NGOs, the public and private sector, in South Africa and around the world. It is also what all the research on organisational behaviour says, very clearly.

---

13 Bolman & Deal, 1997.

I met someone a few years ago who had started a corporate career after being a priest and leading a congregation for ten years. She had been quite nervous about the change, mainly because of the dreadful things she had heard about corporate politics. When I met her a while later, she had realised to her surprise, delight and relief that "corporate politics are *nothing* compared to church politics!"

Another friend who is an academic said to me once that, in universities, "the fights are so vicious because the stakes are so low." (Apparently a quote that is widely used in academic circles all around the world.) The same is true for NGOs, places which exist to "do good" in the world and where the general assumption (or single story) is that only good things happen every day as a result. I am very proud of the work that I have done in civil society and am grateful every day for the good work all kinds of organisations do in this space. But don't kid yourself – charities and NGOs are also riven with politics.

I've mentioned my work with NOAH, and working there remains one of the seminal experiences of my life, not just my career. It was an extraordinary initiative, full of inspirational people and examples of decency, courage and selflessness. It also operated, inevitably, in a context of politics. I remember very clearly getting a call one day that brought this stark reality home.

We had just set up an Ark in a rural area of KwaZulu-Natal and hired the five or six people needed to run the project daily. Jobs are scarce in South Africa, and even more so in rural areas. As such, even with their relatively low salaries, there was a lot of interest in the jobs that we had advertised and background screening was not a normal step, nor plausible. Operations had started, and all seemed to be on track for us to deliver our range of services – providing help, care and support to extremely vulnerable members of our country – to the grandparent- and child-headed households in that area.

A few days in, I received a call from the Ark manager which started innocuously enough.

"Niven, we had a bit of a problem at the Ark this morning."

"Oh dear. What was the problem? Is everything okay?"

And from there, it went, frankly, a little crazy.

"Well, the problem was that a hitman arrived at the Ark to kill the cook."

"WHAT?!"

"No, no, don't worry. It all worked out fine."

"*WHAT?!* How on *earth* could something like that work out fine?!"

"Well, because the cook was the hitman's cousin – something he didn't know when he accepted the hit – and so he obviously didn't kill her…"

While I was absolutely dumbfounded, people with more experience of local community dynamics and politics were not. In the area where we were working, this way of solving problems was not unheard of, or uncommon. What had happened was that the person who did not get the cook's position had hired a hitman to eliminate her "opposition", believing that in so doing, it would pave the way for her to take up the role instead. Talk about informal and unofficial ways to get things done…

Politics are inevitable and inescapable

As a delegate of my seminars once said, with some astonishment as she realised politics' pervasiveness, "We even have politics in our own families. Of *course* we are going to have them at work!" She was right and while there may be all kinds of reasons for this, Bolman and Deal's research puts forward five that make sense:

1. Organisations don't have an independent life or identity. They are actually just the sum of many coalitions, both of individuals and of particular interests, which are always shifting.

2. These individuals and coalitions will always have different views, values, perspectives and perceptions of reality no matter how strong

the vision and sense of purpose in the organisation. (Interestingly, going back to the delegate's insight about family politics, research into relationships by John Gottman PhD shows that 69% of problems in relationships are 'unsolvable'. i.e. they will always be there, no matter what. That doesn't mean that you will spend 69% of your time arguing. If it did, we'd all have to run for the hills now! What it *does* mean is that no matter how much you love and respect your partner, most (69%) of how you see the world is – and will always be – different. Consequently, the trick to a successful relationship is to somehow find ways to manage these differences rather than eliminate them because the latter is merely impossible.[14] If this is true in a marriage, or intimate relationship of two people, how much truer is it going to be in a large organisation with hundreds, or thousands of people?)

3. The most critical decisions in all organisations centre around who gets what, i.e. what resources get allocated to whom. As my first year Economics professor said on the first day of lectures, "economics is all about choosing how to allocate finite resources across infinite demands." The same holds true in organisations.

4. In the same way that organisations don't have separate identities, they also don't have set goals and objectives that are arrived at from a rational process of objective analysis. Instead, they emerge from all kinds of processes of "bargaining, negotiation and jockeying among stakeholders."

5. Put all these different interests across different stakeholders together with scarce resources, and it is almost inevitable that power becomes the most important resource of all to get things done.[15]

If this is true, then, even more so than usual, hope cannot be a strategy. Neither can sticking your head in the sand. In other words, hoping that politics will go away is not a good option if you want to build a successful career. Neither is being an ostrich and thinking that if you keep your head down and just get on with things, that will be enough, and all the politics will pass you by.

---

14 Feuerman, 2017.

15 Bolman & Deal, 1997.

Wherever you are, whatever role you are in, politics are here to stay. And the sooner you can get smart in the playing of them, the better for you, your team, your organisation and your career.

Politics exist on a spectrum

While politics are inevitable, it is vital to understand that there are nevertheless different kinds of political environments in which they play out. Kathleen Kelley Reardon is Professor of Management and Organization in the University of Southern California Marshall School of Business and a leading authority on, among other things, politics in the workplace. She has identified four kinds of political environments that occur, potentially all at the same time in different parts of the organisation. She argues correctly that if you are going to be politically astute, the first thing you need to do is identify what kind of environment you are operating in.

If you are in an environment that is **minimally politicised,** things are typically quite pleasant and easy-going. Conflict is unusual and when it happens, is generally over quickly with no lasting repercussions or hard feelings. It also doesn't feel like there are 'in-groups' and 'out-groups' and 'winners' and 'losers'. Rules can sometimes be bent, and people can do each other favours outside of the regulations, but things like this happen in an atmosphere of trust, respect and regard for the best interests of the organisation. In other words, in these kinds of environments, it's generally a case of good politics at play rather than bad.

As Professor Reardon says though, "these environments are more the exception than the rule." Certainly, in my 20-year career, I've only come across one organisation that I could say fits this description. As such, if this is your perception of your workplace, you could be exceptionally lucky, or out of touch and taking too many mood enhancing supplements. Maybe you're just experiencing a honeymoon moment – for a moment it generally is.

Taking it up a notch, you are in a **moderately politicised** team, department or organisation if there are rules that are commonly understood and generally applied; if the focus is on customers, results, teamwork and trusting each other, and if the politics that exist, serve to deliver what matters to customers rather than to destroy colleagues. In this kind of context, "achieving objectives via unsanctioned methods isn't unusual but tends to be subtle and deniable." Conflict exists more so than in a minimally politicised arena, and it can escalate. However if and when things do get heated, there are shared rules, values and processes for resolving differences effectively. According to Professor Reardon's research, these kinds of environments are more typically found in smaller firms or large ones that put a premium on acting quickly and with agility. In my opinion and experience, both good and bad politics are possible and practised in these environments.

When you are in a team, department or organisation that is **highly politicised** however, conflict is everywhere, even if it is not overt and visible. It is very clear who is part of the 'in-crowd' and who is not. Formal rules, processes and procedures exist only on paper and are used only when convenient to those in power, and very few people are brave (or stupid) enough to communicate directly with senior managers. Instead, things are filtered continuously, and hierarchy and rank are not only important, but feel like a matter of survival. "'Who' is more important than 'what' you know, and work is often highly stressful, especially for those who are in the 'out-groups'. When there's conflict, people rely on aggressive political methods and involve others in the dispute."

In environments like these, leaders become very good at dishing out blame and getting rid of people they see as the problem. This becomes a vicious cycle, because they then never get to the root of problems, focussing instead only on the symptoms. As they see it, these symptoms are inevitably the fault of everyone *but* themselves, not least because they benefit from knowing their way around the intricate politics and constantly use this knowledge to their advantage. Conflicts rarely get raised openly and certainly never get solved. Instead, they simmer and anything or anyone brought in to address this kind of culture is seldom able to do so. Why? Because the organisation doesn't want real, structural changes, but rather quick fixes and someone to blame when these don't work.

Nevertheless, from my experience of having worked in such environments, it is possible to play both good politics and bad politics in them. In fact, good politics become even more critical than usual because politics are the only way that anything meaningful gets done in the organisation.

On the worst end of the political spectrum are **pathologically politicised** organisations which are, frankly and tragically, "often on the verge of self-destruction." Productivity is drastically lower than it should be, not least because people tell those in charge what they want to hear, rather than what they need to and what is actually going on. There is a complete lack of trust between people. Conflict is everywhere and it lasts for a long time. To get things done, people have got to go around the formal rules, processes and procedures and spend a lot of time 'covering their backs' (or other parts of their anatomy). Managers see their role as controlling others rather than encouraging them and working with them, because anyone below them is at best, inferior, and at worst, stupid and useless.

In my opinion and experience, when you are in an environment like this, the only reality is bad politics. Actually, politics become so bad that they – like the environment – are truly toxic.[16]

Identifying political pathology

While such toxic environments are hopefully rare (I have only experienced one in my entire career), they are also undeniably real and deeply damaging all round. Professor Reardon pinpoints a number of signs to look out for to identify an environment that is already pathologically politicised or on the way to becoming so:

---

16 Reardon, 2015.

1. There is **frequent flattery** of the person or group of people in power, while those who are weaker are dismissed, sidelined or even abused.

2. **Information is continuously manipulated** so that anything that might upset those in positions of power is downplayed. Honest and direct communication is rare. Instead, people are constantly on tenterhooks, making sure that they don't do or say anything that will 'rock the boat.'

3. **Vicious gossip and backstabbing** happen all the time, even when things are seemingly polite and professional on the surface.

4. **Indifference and disregard** for people is the order of the day. People are dispensable and disposable, and the best, or only, way to survive is to get to others before they get to you.

5. **Fake left, go right**. In other words, what you see is the complete opposite of what is going on. People deliberately set others up to fail so that *they* can look good by comparison. Hardly surprisingly, teamwork is non-existent and any idea that your colleagues or management 'have your back' is a fantasy. Instead, they are all out to stab you in the back.[17]

What isn't said, but what should be clear to you as you read these points, is that an environment like this is one of debilitating and almost constant fear. As a result, the damage done to people, team, departments and organisations is almost incalculable.

Years ago, I was a police reservist, and received training in domestic abuse. I found the training interesting and valuable but I also couldn't relate to it because I had (and fortunately still have) no experience of emotional abuse in a personal relationship. It was only when I found myself in a truly toxic professional environment that I understood quite how corrosive abuse is and what kind of damage it does. It was the first (and only) time that I worked for a 'snake in a suit'[18] and the physical, emotional and mental toll it took on me, and my colleagues was appalling. The damage done to the institution itself was devastating.

---

17 Reardon, 2015.

18 A term coined by industrial psychologist Paul Babiak PhD and criminal psychologist Robert D. Hare PhD in "Snakes in Suits – When Psychopaths Go To Work", a book that they co-wrote in 2006

I am a self-confident and capable person, with a lot to be proud of. I find huge pleasure and purpose in the work I do, but the impact of that environment was to slowly chip away at all of that until eventually, the only way that I could save myself was to leave. Leaving also made a big difference to my marriage, as I was bringing my frustration, anger and disgust home with me every day, as I found things increasingly unbearable.

I am not alone. When I talk about toxic environments in my lectures, people who have experienced it use words like "shattered", "broken", "believing that I was incapable of anything", "spending five months living at home with my parents again to put the pieces back together."

It is almost as dreadful to hear things like this, as it was to experience them. That is not to say that such experiences can't also be redemptive and teach us an enormous amount. I had a colleague in one organisation who was constantly bullied and belittled by her manager, to the point where she ended up leaving in real distress. She went on to use that experience though as the basis of her PhD on corporate bullying. With a lot of work and dedication, she took what was an awful experience and turned it to her advantage. However, if I had to ask her if it was worth it, I'm not sure she would say that it was.

I know that my experience of toxicity was certainly not worth it. Yes, it was invaluable in giving me empathy for others in similar situations and to remind myself of my values and what I will and will not accept in life. But was it *worth it*? I honestly don't think so.

I have reflected a lot on this experience and all the things I tried to do to fix it, including going to a coach, going directly to the CEO when no-one else would speak up and also going to the whistleblowing line. None of that helped, and in researching the topic of politics and power, I have come to realise that nothing would have resolved this situation. My conclusion is borne from all the research that I have read and that delegates have shared. In a pathologically politicised, or toxic environment like this, the only option is to get out. Get out, one way or another, and sooner rather than later.

I certainly don't say this lightly. I fully understand that in an economy like ours, the reality of being without a job and paycheque is terrifying for many people. So yes, leaving has many consequences. But in my deeply held opinion and experience, staying presents even more risks. At the very least, similarly to domestic abuse, things are in all likelihood only going to get worse, and when it is over, you may not be able to recognise yourself and pick up the pieces of what is left of you, your confidence and your competence.

Being good at politics is critical for your career success

There is an overwhelming amount of research that shows that beyond technical competence, personality and qualifications, it is political intelligence that makes the real difference to career success.[19, 20, 21, 22, 23, 24, 25]

This is hardly surprising if you stop to think about it.

Very few of the real
challenges you face
in work are technical
– most of them are
interpersonal. In an ideal
world, technical skills,
hard work, putting your
head down and just

19   Reardon, 2015.

20   Kaiser, Chamorro-Premuzic & Lusk, 2017.

21   Jarrett, 2017.

22   Spicer, 2014.

23   Todd, Harris & Harris, 2009.

24   Braddy & Campbell, 2014.

25   Wenderoth, 2016.

"getting on with things" would maybe be enough to guarantee that those in power would recognise and reward your contributions. But in the real world, they simply are not.

One of Professor Reardon's books sums this up perfectly and succinctly in its title: "It's ALL politics - Winning in a world where talent and hard work are not enough."

And yet, as Andrew Spicer from Cass Business School puts it so well:

"Executives are smart people, but they can often be remarkably stupid. Too often they assume problems can be solved with superior analytical abilities. This means they spend their time trying to come up with the most rational solution. This might create the best technical solution. However, these technically perfect results often run into stiff opposition and eventually get dropped – so often in favour of an inferior solution. This can be disastrous. It can mean good ideas get shelved, talented managers become frustrated and unmotivated, and organisations get weighed down. Why does this happen? We think the reason behind this is many organisations convince themselves that analytical ability is the only quality that matters. But what is still too often overlooked is political intelligence. This is the understanding of how power and politics work in the organisation."[26]

I realised this very early in my career when I was a consultant at a global strategy consulting firm. It was my first job, and I had a lot to learn. One of my first assignments was a government case. I was the most junior person in a highly skilled team that had been drawn from all over the world

26 Spicer, 2014.

and included subject matter experts, strategy experts and government stakeholders. It was 1998, and South Africa was doing exciting things.

I'm not sure if it is just the haze of nostalgia as I look back more than 20 years ago, but there was a sense of energy and possibility in the years following the 1994 elections. That same sense of collective excitement and dedication permeated this case; one which gave everyone who was part of it, a chance to craft a 20-year strategy for a critical part of the economy. As a result, most of us felt very privileged to be on the team.

After 18 months of rigorous and detailed analysis by experts and stakeholders, the final report was presented to Cabinet, headed at the time by President Nelson Mandela. I was too junior to be in the room during the presentation, but I spoke afterwards to a senior member of the team. I asked him how it had gone and he thought it went rather well. This was not surprising, because we had done exceptional work. It was very clear what the "objectively correct" strategy was for government to follow if it was going to achieve what it had set out to for the country as a whole.

I was very excited to see how it was going to take shape and what impact it was going to have on the country over the next few years. I said as much to my colleague, who took a moment to respond to me. When he did, he said something that has stayed with me ever since: "You know of course though Niven, that the gap between the 'best' and 'most correct' strategy, which is the one that we have just presented and what is *actually* going to happen, is all about power and politics."

He was absolutely right. The strategy we presented was one thing, but what actually happened in the years that followed was different in fundamental ways to what we had put on the table. And this will continue to be the case because, as I've said, politics and power are inescapable.

Marie McIntyre is an organisational psychologist (who knew there was such a thing?) and the head of Executive Counselors, a training and consulting business focused on developing leadership and teamwork in organisations. She has a fabulous website called https://www.yourofficecoach.com/ that offers all sorts of practical career advice. She has also written a great book called *Secrets to Winning at Office Politics*, where she discusses how she surveyed 220 people from various organisations and asked them "When people are good at politics, what are they able to do?"

These were just some of the answers she received:

- Get their projects moved up the priority list
- Influence management
- Have their own office
- Bypass normal procedures
- Advance quickly
- Get asked to solve the toughest problems
- Receive more recognition
- Accomplish results
- Get things done despite significant obstacles
- Get senior management to 'buy-in' on projects
- Help bring about changes
- Get other people to do their work
- Draw attention to a project
- Get more money in their budget
- Acquire resources for their staff
- Stay out of trouble
- Have their ideas heard
- Get raises when other people don't
- Survive changes[27]

Separately to Dr McIntyre's research, the prestigious Center for Creative Leadership (CCL) has spent almost 30 years studying the careers of executives to understand what makes them succeed or derail. They define success and derailment as follows: "Successful executives are those who have reached at least the general manager level and who, in the eyes of senior executives in the organisation, remain likely candidates for promotion. Derailed executives are those who, after reaching the general manager level, are fired, demoted, or held on a career plateau. Right up to the point of derailment, the superiors of the derailed executives saw them as having high potential for advancement, impressive track records, and solidly established leadership positions."[28]

27 McIntyre, 2005.

28 Chappelow & Leslie, n.d.

CCL has found that the two most critical skills that determine success are the ability to build and nurture strong relationships, and the ability to adapt and grow as things change. These skills are at the heart of political intelligence too, and without them, you stand a very good chance of derailing your career, even if you are perfectly technically competent.

In case you are wondering if all this talk of executives means that the political game is only played at a senior level, that is not the case at all. Politics, relationships and power certainly become even more critical to one's career success the more senior we get, but they are a feature of office life at all levels. As such, the sooner we *all* start getting smart about them, the better.

A few years ago, I was speaking to a group of graduates, all newly appointed in the corporate world. One of them started telling the whole group how frustrated she was about the success of another graduate with whom she had attended university and who had received lower marks than she had all through their degree. He had started at the same time as she had, and was doing incredibly well, while she felt stuck. "He's flying and getting all kinds of promotions and opportunities," she said, visibly frustrated and upset. She told us that she had swallowed her pride and asked him what he was doing that was making such a difference to his career trajectory. Her indignation went up at least two notches as she told us his response:

> "I always make sure that my boss knows what I'm doing. And that *her* boss knows what I'm doing."

This young woman was just appalled. "I'm *so* much better than he is at the job and I just want to be recognised for it, instead of having to play politics and suck up to people like he is. It's not fair, it's not right, and it's not who I want to become."

Her reaction did not surprise me. Given all that we've covered about the single negative story of politics, it probably doesn't surprise you either. You may have had precisely the same reaction as her in similar positions, or are having the same reaction right now thinking about her situation. It saddened me, but didn't surprise me that someone so young had such a fixed and rigid idea of what was right and wrong. She almost saw it as a badge of honour that she wasn't playing the same game that he was, even though she was clearly frustrated at being left behind. And of course, her colleague may have been playing all kinds of bad politics, in which case she would have been quite justified in not wanting to emulate him. But that wasn't what she said. As far as I could tell, he was playing perfectly good and legitimate politics, and they were paying dividends for him as a result.

Despite my disappointment at her reaction, I also felt somewhat encouraged. Yes, this young professional had very hard-baked ideas, but she was also only at the start of her career. As such, she still had an opportunity to think and show up differently and by doing so, to take her career to places it might not go if she carried on thinking about power and relationships in the same way. I still think about her and wonder what choices she made...

I hope that by now, you are convinced of how critical it is to be politically smart and that any distinction you (still) make between what we call 'soft' and 'hard' skills is starting to evaporate. Of *course*, we need to be technically skilled – that's a given. The belief that this is going to be enough is a mistake though.

I was still at the South African Reserve Bank in 2014 when the newly appointed Governor, Lesetja Kganyago, addressed all the managers in the auditorium. He spoke passionately and eloquently about the role of the Bank in the country, and I was not the only one who was enormously moved. I don't have a record of his exact words, but the essence of what he said was that as managers we all had a vital role to play in taking care of the people of the bank and making sure that the culture enabled and supported the critical work that its people needed to deliver. He concluded by saying something that I couldn't agree with more when it comes to leadership generally and political intelligence specifically: "No-one must talk to me anymore about these being 'soft' skills. If they are such 'soft' skills, why is it so difficult for all of us to get them right?"

CHAPTER 3

Political and Power Players

"All things are subject to interpretation. Whichever interpretation prevails at a given time is a function of power and not truth."

–Friedrich Nietzsche

As I mentioned in my introduction, I did extensive research on the topic of corporate politics when initially preparing my lectures. It was an invaluable opportunity to get to grips with a subject that I had long avoided and disliked. Once I realised the many aspects and nuances that I hadn't understood previously, it became a very different story. And as my understanding grew, so too did my interest. Office politics is no longer a subject to avoid and roll my eyes at, but one to learn about and engage with. As a result, I continue to learn as much as I can on the topic; partly because of my increased fascination, and partly because of how rewarding it is to be able to teach others and to see the lights come on for them, too.

Unsurprisingly, the more I read, the more models and frameworks I find to explain the types of politics that exist, the kinds of political players there are, the classification of power dynamics, and so on. Many of them are certainly interesting and provide food for thought. Fewer of them are useful in a real-life situation though, and practical utility remains the acid test for what I include in my lectures and in this book.

As a professor of mine once said (quoting the British statistician George E.P. Box), "All models are wrong. Some are just useful". The two that I include here are to my mind useful, because they are more right than wrong. They are drawn from Marie McIntyre's work, which I find very helpful for understanding the concept of corporate politics and more importantly, getting practical about what to do about them.

The difference between wishes and goals

The first of Dr McIntyre's models that I'd like to speak about is our goals and their impact on how we play office politics. She makes an important distinction between a wish and a goal; one that I think is important and bears repeating because it is a distinction that makes a lot of sense when you think about it. However, I had never thought about it, until I read her book.

She says that often we think in terms of wishes, rather than goals. This is especially true when we are having problems, and so we end up saying things like:

"I wish my job paid more."

"I wish that I could get an overseas assignment."

"I wish that I worked for someone I respected."

"I wish that more people in power recognised how much I bring to this company."

As she so correctly points out though, this is not going to get you anywhere.

"Wishing is a passive activity that can easily degenerate into whining and complaining. Goals on the other hand, define the actions we need to take...Wishes put the focus on what we want 'them' to do. Goals highlight what we can do ourselves. Wishes take us out of the power position by implying that we are at the mercy of others. Goals give us power by describing results that we intend to accomplish."[29]

This is a very powerful distinction as you can see if I convert the wishy-washy (pun intended) statements articulated above, into actual goals:

"I am going to get the skills and experience within the next two years that will allow me to get a higher paying job."

"By the end of the month, I will have set up a meeting with the last person who was seconded overseas to ask what they did to make it happen. I am also going to ask them what advice they would give me so that I can do the same."

"I am going to make an effort every day to find at least one thing that my boss did well or that surprised me in a positive way."

---

29   McIntyre, 2005.

"I will make sure that as new assignments come up over the next while, I speak knowledgeably about what I can bring to them. I am also going to offer to take on more than what is strictly required in my actual job by volunteering for extra opportunities as a way of increasing my visibility in the department."

Of course, moving from wishing to planning doesn't guarantee that you will get what you want, but it does require that you do something other than just talk. And by doing something – even if it turns out to be the "wrong" thing – you can move forward and learn. Wishing on the other hand, doesn't teach you anything and it certainly doesn't take you anywhere.

Four types of political players

Many of us have two kinds of goals – personal and business. Personal goals are clearly all about the things you want to achieve for yourself, and these may or may not include work-related goals. They are things like wanting to reach a certain level of management within a certain time, to earn enough to be able to send your children to a particular school, to work with a particular person or in a specific area, to further your development by studying for another degree, to lose weight, to run a marathon, etc. Business goals, by contrast, are about the roles and responsibilities of your position in a team, department and organisation – the things that you are expected to do as an individual and as a colleague to achieve (or exceed) what is required of you in your role.

Marie McIntyre's four political types are classified by how their behaviour impacts personal and business goals. There are several things I like about this model, but what I find particularly valuable is the fact that it focusses on behaviour, which is, after all, the only thing we are judged on. Our intentions are an important starting point, but they are largely invisible to others and sometimes even invisible to ourselves. Intentions only become 'visible' to others through how we act, behave, or 'show up'. It's our behaviour that people see and what they can go on – not what we say, or what we intend, or what we hope for.

	Your behaviour **helps** *your personal goals*	Your behaviour **harms** *your personal goals*
Your behaviour helps the *business goals*	**Winner**	**Martyr**
Your behaviour **harms** the *business goals*	**Sociopath**	**Dimwit**

Figure 1: Four types of political players[30]

According to this model, you are acting like a **dimwit** when you behave in a way that is both self-destructive *and* damaging to your team or organisation. Unsurprisingly, this is the least effective kind of politics and the least effective type of political player to be. There is no upside to this behaviour for anyone – least of all you.

Sociopaths, by contrast, can often do quite well out of their behaviour. Their actions often cause all kinds of fear and contempt, but they can seem (and for a long time *be*), untouchable. As a result, they can look like they are on a fast track to success. However, in my experience, their runway eventually ends and the impact of who they are and what they have done, catches up with them.

This is what eventually happened with the 'snake in a suit' who created the toxic environment I mentioned previously. He had cut a swathe of destruction and fury wherever he worked, including in the organisation where we worked together. It was appalling to watch and when he left for an even bigger role in an important organisation elsewhere, we could only pity the poor souls on whom his incompetence and arrogance were going to be unleashed next. Much to my relief, and the delight of very many people who had had the misfortune of having to work with him, he was finally caught out and publicly fired in an organisation-wide shake-up and clean-up.

---

30   McIntyre, 2015.

Martin Luther King said it beautifully: "The arc of the moral universe is long, but it bends towards justice."

Martyrs are seemingly the kind of committed staff that we should all aspire to be. They are enormously dedicated to the organisation and will do whatever they can to help it succeed. Without question, professional commitment is admirable and necessary. But when it is taken to this extreme, it often comes at quite a significant personal cost, because martyrs are masters at ignoring what matters to them personally. (Assuming that they even know what matters to them of course.) Eventually, however, even though it is a situation of their own making, they can start to feel a lot of resentment at always putting themselves last.

Taken further though, the end result can be even worse than resentment. I am reminded of a story that was told to me by an investment banker, a delegate at one of my lectures. When we spoke about martyrs, she told us the story of a woman (let's call her Mary) that she had once worked with, who fitted this bill exactly. Mary was totally committed to her job and took huge pride in always being on call and being the first to cancel holidays if needed, to help out at work.

Note that I said 'always'. In other words, this wasn't about the kinds of situations we have all had to deal with – ones of immovable deadlines, huge pressure and all hands on deck to deliver something urgent and critical. Those kinds of intense projects or very concentrated bursts of stress are unavoidable sometimes, but should not be a permanent condition of work. However, Mary's way of working had become habitual, so that no matter how important or unimportant, urgent or not things were, she was always there, putting the bank first and herself last.

The woman telling the story said that she remembered admiring Mary hugely and thinking what an asset she was. She also remembered wondering how they would replace her if she ever decided to leave, given the critical role she played in the team. She then went on to tell us how a few years ago, Mary was at work on Christmas Eve and, as per usual, putting in a full day. She stayed home on Christmas Day, but the next day (26 December) she was back at work, at her desk again, which is where she was found by a security guard. Mary had died at her desk.

Clearly, this part of the story was distressing for all of us to hear and for Mary's colleague to tell. What made it even more upsetting though was that Mary, this apparently irreplaceable, one-of-a-kind professional, was in fact replaced within a few days. There was someone else seated at her desk before the new calendar year started.

I would therefore urge you to think very carefully about the choices you are making in your career and the rest of your life, particularly when it comes to the things you want to achieve in your personal life that you are sacrificing for work. I say this as someone who takes enormous pride and pleasure in the work I do (I may have mentioned that). Work gives my life meaning, direction and purpose, and so a considerable part of my pleasure in life comes from work. At the same time, though, work is just one aspect of my life, and I am very clear on that.

The same may be true for you too, but would anyone know it from your behaviour and how you are showing up politically at work? If your life is all about the organisation you work for, and everyone knows that, maybe people do see you as dedicated and exceptional. Is it possible though, that you are also seen as a diligent and docile doormat?

Winners, in my experience and according to Dr McIntyre's research, are the ones who really come out on top of the political career game over the long term. And it's hardly surprising, because their behaviour helps them to achieve their goals, but in such a way that their organisation benefits too. I can think of several people I admire who fit this bill. They are people I feel fortunate to have been able to work with, who have left me feeling hugely enriched and who I have learnt a huge amount from. And they have made the same impact in their organisations.

While Marie McIntyre classifies these as four separate political archetypes, she also makes the point that we all move between the various quadrants. Different contexts, stresses and stressors inevitably bring out the best and the worst in us. I have certainly seen that in myself and as a result, have learnt, painfully, the important lesson of recognising what triggers the best and worst versions of myself, so that I can (try to) modify my behaviour accordingly.

Of course, this is easier said than done for something that is a lifelong discipline and practice. The first step in this journey of mastery is awareness; awareness of the triggers and situations that 'press my hot buttons' and make me behave like a real fool, and those that give me the opportunities to lead, inspire, shine and (apologies for the cliché) 'be my best self'.

In conclusion, Dr McIntyre puts it well. "Those who consistently behave like Martyrs, Sociopaths or Dimwits are doomed to eventual failure and disappointment. Their political power is automatically limited by their excessive behaviour, which gradually alienates everyone around them. Although most of us are not so extreme, we all act out of bitterness, selfishness or uncontrolled emotion from time to time. Sadly, these destructive tendencies prevent many people from reaching their full potential as Winners."[31]

Different types of power

I've made the point a few times now that politics is all about relationships, perceptions and power. As such, while it is important to understand the kind of political player you are being, relative to the kind you want to be (and want to be seen as), it is equally important to understand what kind of power player you are showing up as. To do that, it is useful to first understand a bit more about the concept of power itself. It is too often misunderstood and – just like corporate politics – shied away from, because power is also often seen as only one kind of story, and certainly not a story that we can talk about openly. Can you even imagine an environment where people just came right out and said, "I want more power," or, "Why do you have so much power?" Even better – "I really enjoy having power over you and all your colleagues."

In the mind's eye, this is almost laughably impossible, yet power is inescapably part of the reality of every organisation. To navigate it, we must understand it. There are many ways to classify and understand power because it is a concept that has been researched and analysed for years. The most enduring studies on power were done over 70 years ago when two social psychologists, John French and Bertram Raven, described five

---

31   McIntyre, 2005.

bases of positional power and then a few years later added a sixth. Each of the six types they identify falls into one of two categories – positional or personal power.

Positional power is the authority that you have because of your position in an organisation's structure and hierarchy, and it includes four sources:

1. Legitimate power – This is the power that a person has because others believe that they have the right to it. By definition, it correlates to the particular position that a person holds, what is expected or assumed of that position, and the appropriateness of the process that put the person into that position. For example, a properly appointed Head of Audit in an organisation has the legitimate power to audit and pass judgement on the soundness of how that organisation's financials are presented. Their role gives them the legitimacy to do this. A personal assistant or the Head of Corporate Services would clearly *not* have the same kind of legitimate power when it comes to passing authorised judgement on an organisation's financials. They *would* have legitimate power to act in accordance with *their* role and *it's* rights and responsibilities. Legitimate power is a very unstable source of power, because the moment a person is no longer in the position that gave them their legitimate power, they can find themselves with very little – if any – power at all. How many of us have seen this play out very sadly when people retire? They were so closely identified, with their position or title, by themselves and others, that they quite literally don't know who they are when they no longer occupy those roles.

2. Reward – This power comes from the ability of one person (A) to compensate another (B) if B does what A requires. This compensation can come in many forms, such as an increase, a promotion, or an award, etc. The form that the reward takes is irrelevant. What matters is that A can make sure that B is rewarded if B complies and that B is *not* rewarded if they don't. This is the typical power that a manager has over a subordinate who relies on that manager for their performance review, assessment and bonus. Even if it is mediated by a forum of other managers and subject to the rules, policies and constraints of the organisation and its finances, we all know that it is the immediate manager who has the most power to sway these decisions.

3.   Coercive – This is the power that you have when others believe (or know) that you will punish them if they don't do as you say. There is a time and a place to use all of the six powers but this one, relying as it does on threats and punishments, should be avoided unless there is absolutely no other option. It can very quickly erode the goodwill and trust of those you who are wanting to lead or influence. The result of over-using this power is that while you may get compliance – grudging or otherwise – you certainly will not get true followership.

4.   Informational – You get tremendous power when you have access to, or control over, information that others need or want. Knowing about retrenchments before other people do, knowing who is in line for promotions, knowing what the executive said about someone's project in a closed meeting and so on are all examples of informational power. It is a particularly significant power that "derives not from the information itself but from having access to it, and from being in a position to share, withhold, manipulate, distort, or conceal it. With this type of power, you can use information to help others, or as a weapon or a bargaining tool against them."[32] Sole access to information amongst a group of co-workers obviously leads to opportunities to withhold or alter that information.

Personal power is the power you have by virtue of who you are – your individual, personal ability to influence people and events, irrespective of the formal authority you have or have not been given. It comes from your character, your personality, your ethics and your life experiences. It is unique to you. According to French and Raven's research, personal power comprises two sources, namely:

5.   Expert – This power comes from being a subject matter expert, either as a result of years of experience and/or because of formal, academic qualifications in a particular field. Irrespective of which of these is the source of an expert's power, people acknowledge them as someone who 'knows what they are talking about' and defer to them accordingly. Expert power, precisely because it is personal power, is something that cannot be taken away from anyone. That does not mean, however, that people who have expert power will always have

---

32   Mindtools, 2019.

it if their knowledge falls behind or becomes redundant, especially in a world that is changing as rapidly and continuously as ours is.

6.   Referent – Referent power is fundamental, because it has to do with how others perceive you and the degree to which people like, admire, trust and respect you as a person. If you have a lot of referent power, people generally want to do what you need and ask. If you don't, they don't. It is one of the most critical powers to develop and one of the most important to use to your advantage and the advantage of your team and organisation. That said, "referent power can be a big responsibility because you don't necessarily have to do anything to earn it. So, it can be abused quite easily. Someone who is likeable, but who lacks integrity and honesty, may rise to power and use that power to hurt and alienate people as well as to gain personal advantage. Relying on referent power alone is not a good strategy for a leader who wants longevity and respect."[33]

Ultimately, the most critical thing to understand about power is that anyone can have it and anyone can influence others. It is most definitely not something that only sits with a few people who have impressive-sounding titles or corner offices.

---

33   Mindtools, 2019.

Instead, it is about recognising the different types of power that exist so that you can draw on all of them as needed, to make yourself the most effective and influential political player possible. Knowing the different types that others can draw on, also allows you to understand when people around you are trying to abuse their power, so you can take the appropriate steps to block them and protect yourself.

Developing a power grid for your environment

When it comes to being a political player, you need to be able to assess and understand all the various kinds of power and to know what to do about them practically. Dr McIntyre's power grid, with its four combinations, is a useful way to think about your own power, as well as how power is playing out in your environment.

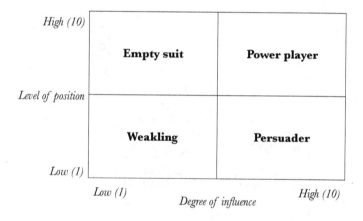

Figure 2: Power Grid (McIntyre, 2005)

Politically speaking, those on the left of her grid don't have much power. You can recognise people with limited power in several ways, including that they are probably:

- Not doing important work
- Talking a lot about the past
- Trying to sound more important than they are
- Dropping names of important people
- Liking to spend most of their time alone

- Having little interest in their work
- Avoiding conflict or handling it poorly

When you combine a low level of influence with a low-level position, you have what she calls **weaklings** – people who may be perfectly nice and perfectly competent, but who don't have much impact or recognition outside of their actual job and what they are there to do. By contrast, **empty suits** have high-level positions with impressive titles and so they seemingly have more influence. In reality though, they also have very limited power and influence, if any. In fact, McIntyre says that "these are the jobs where politically ineffectual executives go to die."[34] Clearly, neither of these is a place in which you want to find yourself if you are trying to get better at organisational politics.

I have certainly seen empty suits and weaklings in organisations where I have worked. I didn't classify them as such at the time, given my political naivety. I remember one executive in particular, who was the epitome of an empty suit. His title, when I first joined the company, was extremely impressive, as was he when I first met him. He had years of experience and lots of degrees and was also just a very nice and sincere person. However, it didn't take long for me to realise that he was literally just wandering the corridors, desperate for someone – anyone – to speak to. He was senior and important enough that he wouldn't be asked to leave, but that was about all when it came to influence. The organisation's leaders were really just waiting for him to retire, and keeping him out of any meaningful decisions or work until he did.

Nice as they may be on the personal front, people on the left-hand side of the grid generally don't have enough power to be a professional ally worth having or worth cultivating, relative to all the other allies you could or should be making. Furthermore, anyone on the left-hand side who looks like they are heading for political suicide (more on this later), should be avoided. You need to keep your distance from someone who is self-destructing publicly and make very sure that your reputation does not get tainted by association.

---

34   McIntyre, 2005.

When it comes to boosting your own power, you need to move yourself into the right part of the grid and put your effort into cultivating relationships with those colleagues who you have identified to be in this space, i.e. the so-called **persuaders** and **power players. Persuaders** are also called "opinion leaders" because while they don't feature prominently on the organogram, they can and do influence a lot of people. The classic example here is Personal Assistants (PAs) and Executive Assistants (EAs). Anyone with any experience of organisations knows how powerful PAs are and how much easier your life becomes if they like you – not to mention how the exact opposite is true if they do not.

The other people who I have found to be very good persuaders are those with strong institutional knowledge. They may not be particularly senior, but they know everyone and everything and they are invaluable in helping you find an easier or better way to get things done. Whatever positions they hold, the reality is that persuaders "are probably your most useful allies because they are fairly accessible. It's easier to chat with the CEO's assistant than with the CEO."[35]

Power players are the ones who, as McIntyre puts it, "truly run the show." If you are not a power player yourself and don't wish to be one, then at the very least you should be identifying who the power players are, so you can make them your allies. And if that is not possible, then you need to make sure that you at least don't antagonise them. I am *not* talking here about turning a blind eye to criminal or unethical behaviour. That's when the political rules need to go out the window in the interests of a bigger concern. What I'm talking about is not doing stupid, unnecessary things that will get you on the wrong side of the people who hold this kind of political power.

35   McIntyre, 2005.

In conclusion

All models are simply a representation of reality – they are not reality itself. As such, there are always going to be complexities and exceptions to any picture we have, and this is particularly true when it comes to the idea of people being political weaklings.

I was told a story a few years ago, which ever since, has informed my own approach to leadership, problems and opportunities. Told to me by an extraordinarily successful business woman, it was about a period when, for family reasons, she needed to hand the company that she and her husband had built from scratch, over to an interim CEO.

For months, everything seemed to be working out as well as she could have hoped for. However, leaving the offices one day after her weekly meeting with the acting CEO, a cleaning lady approached and asked for a few minutes of her time. The cleaning lady said that she wanted to show her something. The woman who told me the story emphasised how her first (unspoken) reaction to her cleaning lady was, "Not now, I'm running late. Can't it wait?"

Despite this inward impatience, she humoured the employee, following her from the main office into the warehouse that formed part of the extended business premises. As she entered the warehouse, the business owner was stopped in her tracks by the sight of inventory that, wherever she looked, reached to the ceiling. This was very obviously a significant and serious problem – not just because of stock-control issues, but because the reality of what she was seeing bore absolutely no relation to the figures on paper that she had been examining a few minutes previously.

In a nutshell, the acting CEO had been engaging in fraud that was so widespread, the company was in imminent danger of collapse. The owner was left with no option but to take charge and re-mortgage all of her properties to raise sufficient capital to rescue her business. She ended up bringing the company back from the brink so successfully that it was sold to a multinational a few years ago for a substantial sum.

The businesswoman told me that the moral of the story for her, was that "you *never* know where your next best piece of advice is going to come from. My cleaning lady saved my company that day, and she saved me."

I certainly take that moral out of the story too, but to my mind there are two more. The first is that the woman who told me the story had succeeded in creating a company where a cleaning lady cared enough about where she worked to look up from her daily job of sweeping floors and recognise that something was not right. That cleaning lady's job was ostensibly "just to clean", but she did so much more than that. The second moral for me, is that the company was one where a cleaning lady could, and did, go straight to the founding CEO to get her attention about something she could neither explain nor fully understand, but which she knew mattered. And… the founding CEO listened.

How many of us can say that through how we show up at work every day, we are creating an organisation like this? There is no question that power is a fundamental and critical thing to understand. However we do ourselves a disservice if we only cultivate those relationships on the right-hand side of the grid because we think that these people are the only ones worth knowing in work or in life. People on the left-hand side of the grid have intrinsic value as human beings; sometimes far more than we take the time and trouble to realise. It is fundamental that all of us in positions of influence never forget that, and that we create the space for individuals to develop and contribute.

If you find *yourself* on the left-hand side of the grid, the exact same is and remains true of you – whether or not you decide to try and shift your position on the grid going forward, your intrinsic value as a human being remains undiminished.

In closing:

Don't confuse power with authority. Companies may appoint

managers, but it's
employees who decide
if those managers are
leaders.

Exercise: How much power do you have?[36]

Think of someone you regard as a role model for exercising power and influence wisely. Now compare yourself to that person in the areas listed below. Use the following scale:

3 = Definitely   **2 = Somewhat**   **1 = Not Really**

Me			A Power Builder	My Role Model		
3	2	1	Has responsibility for results that are perceived as valuable	3	2	1
3	2	1	Is included in, or consulted about, important decisions	3	2	1
3	2	1	Is allowed to make independent decisions about their work	3	2	1
3	2	1	Has information or skills perceived as valuable by management	3	2	1
3	2	1	Has contact with many people in many parts of the organisation	3	2	1
3	2	1	Is trusted with confidential information	3	2	1
3	2	1	Is involved in important projects	3	2	1

---

36 McIntyre, 2005.

Me			A Power Builder	My Role Model		
3	2	1	Has expertise that is hard to replace	3	2	1
3	2	1	Is listened to by others when speaking	3	2	1
3	2	1	Appears confident and self-assured	3	2	1
3	2	1	Is well regarded by people at all levels	3	2	1
3	2	1	Turns disagreements into productive discussions	3	2	1
3	2	1	Conveys interest and enthusiasm about work	3	2	1
3	2	1	Includes other people in decisions and activities	3	2	1

Moving from assessment to action:

- Look at the items on which you gave yourself a low rating. What could you do to increase your score in that area? If you scored your role model highly on any of those items, what can you learn from that person's behaviour? Might he or she agree to become a coach or mentor for you?
- Think about the power players in your organisation. List the results, values and behaviours that seem to be rewarded by this group. Remember to consider what they *do*, not what they say. Do you need to make changes to be perceived more positively by power players? If most of their values and priorities don't match your own, are you in the right organisation?

CHAPTER 4

How to Become Better
at Office Politics

"We have so much room for improvement. Every aspect of our lives must be subjected to an inventory... of how we are taking responsibility."

–Nancy Pelosi

In 2005, Gerald Ferris[37] and a group of colleagues developed a questionnaire that they called the "Political Skill Inventory" and which they used to measure... wait for it... people's political skill in a workplace. Their research confirmed what has been found in other sources and what was highlighted in Chapter 2 – that leaders who scored highly on political skill were more effective leaders in their organisations and, as a result, less anxious in how they showed up. Their skill came mainly from being able to do two things well at the same time. Firstly, they could ensure good interactions between team members. Secondly, they built a positive reputation for themselves in the organisation.

Ferris and his colleagues also found that, while political skill and emotional intelligence are linked, political skill and IQ are not linked. In other words, you can be intellectually gifted and technically skilled but have no political skill, and vice-versa. Given how much understanding Ferris's work added to the subject of political savviness, a lot of the subsequent writing and research about political intelligence refers back to and builds on it. [38] [39]

---

37   Ferris, 2005.

38   Kaiser, Chamorro-Premuzic & Lusk, 2017.

39   Braddy & Campbell, 2014.

Ferris's work identified four practices that people who are good at politics rely on. While they are separated out conceptually, in reality the practices are very closely linked and reinforce each other continuously. Ultimately, everything that Ferris and his team discovered boiled down to the fact that "politically skilled leaders are adept at reading others' behaviours and motives, influencing others to achieve important goals, building diverse relationship networks and interacting genuinely and sincerely with others. These skills enable leaders to maximise and leverage their relationships in order to get things done efficiently and effectively at work."[40]

Bill Clinton famously said in his successful 1992 presidential campaign, "It's the economy, stupid."

When it comes to political intelligence, I can only say, "It's the people, stupid."

Given that politics and organisations are all about people and human nature, a hard truth to accept is that things are not always going to be fair. Life *should* be fair. The best people *should* be recognised for their commitment and contribution without having to tell everyone about it.

We spend a lot of time contemplating many "shoulds". But this is simply not the way the world works, and it is not likely to change. This is a difficult reality to accept, but it is critical that we do. In Chapter 2, I highlighted the inescapable reality that organisations are and always will be hierarchies

---

40   Braddy & Campbell, 2014.

(experiments with concepts like holacracy notwithstanding). To reinforce the points made there, "the social science bears out uncomfortable truths about politics and interpersonal relationships: We make initial snap judgments of people, often based on appearance, that can carry on over time; we favour those who are similar to us; we get promoted or gain valuable information by making our boss feel good and building relationships with influential people; we form perceptions based on a speaker's appearance, body language and voice more than the content of the argument; and we are more likely to be perceived as competent if we are judiciously critical or show anger. There is strong evidence that our work ratings, bonuses, and promotions are weakly correlated to actual performance – in fact, performance may even matter *less* to our success than our political skills and how we are perceived by those who make the decisions."[41]

Political Skill Self-assessment

Let's start with you and see how high – or low – your political skill currently is. The exercise below is an adapted, mini version of the full questionnaire used in Ferris's[42] research and was developed by the CCL for research they conducted in 2014.

DO I...

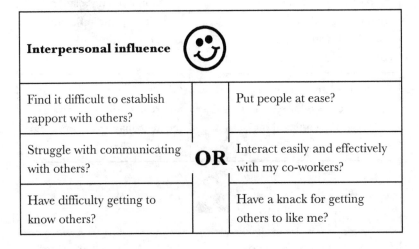

Interpersonal influence		
Find it difficult to establish rapport with others?	OR	Put people at ease?
Struggle with communicating with others?	OR	Interact easily and effectively with my co-workers?
Have difficulty getting to know others?	OR	Have a knack for getting others to like me?

---

41   Wenderoth, 2016.

42   Ferris, 2005.

Social awareness		
Focus primarily on my own agenda and myself?		Try to understand the motives behind other people's actions?
Struggle with knowing how to present myself to others?	**OR**	Consistently make positive impressions on others?
Struggle with having small talk or carrying on conversations?		Naturally know the right things to say to influence others in most situations?
Networking ability		
Stay to myself and spend virtually all of my time at work completing job-related tasks?		Deliberately spend time networking with others at work?
Primarily spend time with a close group of coworkers and friends with whom I feel comfortable?	**OR**	Invest in building relationships with diverse and influential people at work?
Almost exclusively rely on formal processes for securing resources and getting things done?		Often leverage my networks and relationships at work to secure valuable resources and get things done?
Apparent Sincerity		
Only show interest in others when I need something from them?		Take time to regularly show genuine interest in people at work?

Come across as being manipulative because I say and do what is needed to get what I want?	**OR**	Act sincerely around others?
Have a tendency to be very secretive and to keep people on a strict 'need to know' basis?		Communicate openly and transparently with others?

If your answers tended to be in the right-hand column, it would seem that you are already practising political skills successfully. If your answers tended to be in the left-hand column, then you probably have some room for sharpening your political skills, which is precisely what this chapter is about. So let's get to it.

Interpersonal influence

Interpersonal influence is simply about being able to affect what and how other people think. However, this kind of influence starts with wanting to understand other people and what matters to *them*. Only then can you find ways to influence them; ways that convince them based on how they see the world.

How many of us were taught as children to 'treat others as you would want to be treated?' Actually, in many instances (and certainly when it comes to political intelligence) the opposite is true – we should be treating others as they want to be treated. Doing this requires curiosity and interest, but it also demands that you put your own ego and perceptions to one side. And that is something that doesn't always come naturally to us.

As much as I enjoy my own company, I get a lot of pleasure from engaging with other people. Consequently, any personality profile tests I have taken tag me as an 'ambivert' – a combination of an introvert and an extrovert. People often misunderstand both of these terms, seeing introverts as shy and unassuming, and extroverts as loud and confident. In fact, the definition is dependent on where you get your energy from, rather than how much energy and exuberance you display. Introverts get their energy from themselves and extroverts from other people. Ambiverts veer between the two.

As a result, I have always believed that I have a good way with people, and generally, that is true. When it comes to the kind of strategic interpersonal influence that is required to be politically smart though, I have found that learning and understanding more about relationship types and managing stakeholders has been a significant eye-opener. It's not just about liking people and enjoying their company. Getting politically smart requires that we go deeper than that, with others and with ourselves.

Avoiding the fundamental attribution error

I was taught an interesting concept by one of my professors, and it has stayed with me throughout my life:

"We judge ourselves by our intentions and others by their impact."

No doubt you too can think of times where a conversation or interaction didn't work out in the way that you had intended and you offended, irritated, or hurt someone. And you (like many of us) were really taken aback at how your very good intentions were so badly received, protesting with "I didn't mean that". "What I was trying to do was…" Only to have the other person's response be something along the lines of, "I don't care what you meant. This is what it felt/sounded like…"

The same is true when it comes to the concessions we make for ourselves relative to the concessions we *don't* make for others. This behaviour has a name – the fundamental attribution error. Patrick Lencioni, author of "Five Dysfunctions of a Team", explains it perfectly. "Human beings tend to falsely attribute the negative behaviours of others to their character (an internal attribution) while they attribute their own negative behaviours to their environment (an external attribution). Why? Because we like to believe that we do bad things because of the situations we are in, but somehow we easily come to the conclusion that others do bad things because they are predisposed to being bad. (Similarly, we often attribute other people's success to their environment and our own success to our character. That's because we like to believe that we are inherently good and talented, while others are merely lucky, beneficiaries of good fortune.)"[43]

Understanding relationship types

Jocelyn Davis is a leading thinker and writer on the subject of leadership, and her work on relationship types is particularly interesting. She says that "we tend to think of relationships as falling along a single dimension, from friend to enemy…This view is inadequate. Relationships should, in fact, be arrayed along not one but two dimensions: whether the person is with you or against you; and whether that stance is conditional or unconditional."[44]

If you do this exercise, you will find four main relationship types: Friends, Foes, Allies and Adversaries.

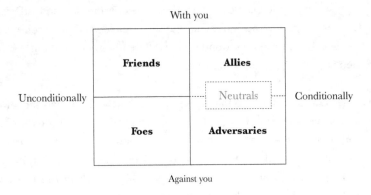

Figure 3: Relationship types[45]

Friends, as the diagram shows, are those people who are unconditionally with you – on your side, no matter what. **Foes** are those colleagues who are unconditionally against you, irrespective of what you do, or will ever do. By contrast, **Allies** and **Adversaries** support you or don't, depending on

---

43 Lencioni, 2005.

44 Davis, 2016.

45 Davis, 2016.

whether it suits them and their interests. So their position – be it supportive or otherwise – is conditional. As such, by definition, if adversaries' conditions can be met, they can be converted to allies, while if allies' conditions are not met, they can become neutrals or adversaries.

When I saw this model, I realised a few important things. The first was that I have actually had far fewer foes than I thought I did throughout my career. I had lost opportunities for traction and momentum by dismissing some people out of hand unnecessarily, frustrated that 'they just didn't get it and didn't want to get it.' What I could have and should have been doing was taking the time and trouble to understand how these people saw things and then seeing how I could get them on my side.

With hindsight, many of them were probably what Davis calls 'Allies in waiting'. If I had realised that their resistance was conditional, and that it was well within my power to meet those conditions, I could well have had them on my side. None of the conditions were unethical or illegal, just *different* from what I had understood about respective situations. Having these colleagues on my side could have made things enormously more effective for me, my team and the organisation. Instead, I alienated these colleagues unnecessarily and can only wonder how differently some things may have turned out, knowing what I know now.

The second important realisation was that I had actually had far fewer friends at work than I thought I did. And that was really no bad thing. Friends in life are wonderful, but in a political and work situation, they are less important than allies. We don't go to work to make friends. If and when we do end up making a few that last beyond our working relationships, fabulous. What we should be doing at work is to build positive relationships with as many allies as possible, because it is allies and alliances that enable us to get things done. Allies are on your side because you have the same goals. It's a mistake to confuse the two and an unnecessary waste of energy to try to make colleagues into friends when what you really need are allies. Understanding this is critical to developing political intelligence.

In one of her books, Jocelyn Davis recounts a scene from the TV series *Downton Abbey* that I remember watching. In the scene, the character Cora, Countess of Grantham, tries to get the help of her mother-in-law, the wonderfully formidable Dowager Countess played by Maggie Smith. The two women are very different in many ways and as a result, have several disagreements throughout the series. In this particular instance, the Dowager Countess says that she is prepared to help Cora. Grateful and happy, Cora breathes a big sigh of relief, smiles, looks at her mother-in-law and says, "So we're friends?" To which her mother-in-law replies, "*Allies*, my dear. Which are far more useful."[46]

Managing stakeholders

Like me, you may have been in situations or projects where you have had to draw up a stakeholder matrix at the start. This is where you list all the stakeholders whose input to, and awareness of, a project matters. When I have had to do this, it was usually for reasons of governance more than anything. We always needed to show that we had done things properly, and part of doing things properly was to conduct a stakeholder analysis. There are all kinds of ways to classify stakeholders. The one that I have used below is the last matrix in the book – I promise.

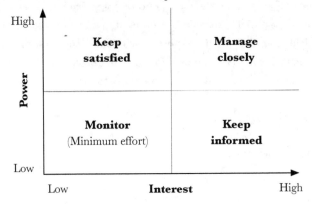

Figure 4: Generic stakeholder matrix

If you are anything like me, your lists of stakeholders were then shelved, never to be formally referred to or thought through again. What a mistake! Managing your stakeholders, deliberately and strategically is a vital part of being politically intelligent. It was something that I didn't fully understand and utilise for far too long in my career, and completely unlike a very smart, very successful woman I met a few years ago.

---

46   Davis, 2016.

Barely over 40 at the time, she headed up a significant business unit and was on the Executive Committee, i.e. in the top six of an organisation with over 50 000 employees. This woman was respected, well regarded and very impressive, personally and professionally, and she told me something that I found quite revelational. Ever since she had started her career, she had made a point of mapping and managing her stakeholders. Every month, she would sit and deliberately think through the stakeholders that she needed to manage closely, keep informed, keep satisfied or simply monitor. Based on her review, she then used the rest of the month to either set up a lunch with them, invite them to a presentation or drop them an email updating them on the status of an important initiative. Basically, this savvy political player did whatever it took to make sure that they were as updated or 'on board' as they needed to be. She then repeated the process of analysis and action the next month, and the next, and the next, and had done so for over 20 years.

For this woman, 'stakeholder management' was not an abstract concept or a once-off thing that she got around to doing when and if she had the time, or when and if she could be bothered to make the effort. Instead, it was a deliberate and continuous practice; one that she prioritised as much as her 'real work' and had done so for all of her professional life. Suddenly, her enormous success made even more sense to me.

Exercise: Getting the support and allies you need[47]

1. Ask yourself the following questions:

    •   Whose support do I need to achieve my goals at work at the moment and going forward?
    •   Are all of these people in my current network of allies?
    •   If I don't have the allies I need, what has stopped me from developing them?

        o   Maybe you haven't seen their importance?
        o   Maybe you don't know them and don't know how to get to know them in a way that doesn't feel 'fake'?
        o   Maybe you don't like them?

---

47 McIntyre, 2005.

If You Don't Do Politics, Politics Will Do You

Whatever your reason for not having them as an ally, you need to get over it, and you need to get over yourself. You don't have to like someone else to be able to achieve your goals, but you may need to have them on your side.

2. Now draw up two lists

- The first list must include the names of people that need to be your allies and with whom you don't have any relationship at the moment.
- The second must have the names of people that you need to have as allies, but who are currently adversaries.

3. What are the specific things you could do to develop or improve relationships with people on both lists? (Remember to think in terms of goals, over which you have control, not wishes that depend on the other person).

Development Activities identified by CCL[48]

Political Skill	Development Activities	Why Is This Important?
Interpersonal Influence	• Ask more questions and be prepared to actively listen to others. Be sure that others know they are being heard. • Have one-on-one conversations with others that de-emphasise any power dynamics. Try to have conversations in a neutral location rather than in someone's office. This may help to put others at ease and increase their receptivity to your ideas.	Co-workers may want to know that they are being heard and understood, and asking questions and listening are effective tools to integrate into your interpersonal style. CCL's work with senior leaders has shown that friendliness and affability are some of their lowest rated characteristics, and that simply displaying warmth and inquiring about others are powerful ways to build relationship capital, which can be used later to make progress on current and future challenges.

---

48 Braddy & Campbell, 2014.

Political Skill	Development Activities	Why Is This Important?
Interpersonal Influence (Continued)	• Don't underestimate the power of being affable and friendly with others. Try to learn more about others by talking to them about personal and professional interests. Also, be prepared to reveal more about yourself. This will enhance your likeability and help you establish rapport and connections with others, which ultimately will increase your ability to influence others.	The top-down, command-and-control style of communication is losing its effectiveness and is being replaced by a more engaging, person-to-person conversational model that is built on gaining trust, listening, and knowing employees on a more personal level.[49]
	• Sell others on your ideas rather than forcing your idea on them. Help them understand how they will personally benefit from taking your suggestions.	
	• Communicate clearly and concisely with others. When having formal meetings, jot down the specific points you want to make. When relevant, close meetings by drafting specific action items. This will help ensure that there is shared understanding and agreement, and thus builds in accountability for all involved parties.	

Social awareness

Social astuteness refers to the ability to read other people and to understand how they see you. "Most people think of self-awareness as introspection, but its essence is actually other-awareness; that is, knowing how other people see you and how your behaviour impacts them."[50] It's this kind of awareness that allows us to modify how we show up in front of others.

---

49   Groysberg & Slind, 2012.

50   Kaiser, Chamorro-Premuzic & Lusk, 2017.

That is very easy to confuse with being shallow and changeable depending on your audience and the situation. I am not talking about the kind of chameleon behaviour that really is lacking in integrity. Rather, I'm talking about adapting your behaviour to get yourself and your message across most effectively; about keeping your goals front and centre and behaving in a way that will give you the best chance of achieving them. Social awareness essentially requires that instead of taking situations and people at face value, we go a level deeper in assessing, understanding and navigating what is really going on around us.

Understanding the leverage equation

One of the most important things that you need to be good at if you want to improve your political intelligence is to understand the existence and dynamics of the leverage equation. This exists in all relationships, personal and professional, and is really about the power (or leverage) that you have to get others to do what you want. It is something we are all familiar with even if we've never heard the term itself, because if you think about it, most of our interactions, conversations and transactions involve leverage in one way or another.

Here are a few examples:

- You want to attend an overseas conference and have the company pay for it. Is your manager more likely to give it to you if
  a) you've been working really hard on a project for the last few months, one which was critical and had huge success, or
  b) if she had to call you into her office recently to point out that you have been consistently underperforming on tasks allocated to you?

  Obviously the answer is a. That's because your good performance has given you some leverage. It obviously doesn't guarantee you anything, but it does give you something to negotiate with, overtly or implicitly.

- You need a colleague's help on a big assignment. Are they more likely to help you if

a) s/he is going to need your help soon too
b) s/he feels that you have a habit of undermining him/her
c) the two of you are vying for the same promotion?

Again, the answer is fairly clearly a and again, that's because of leverage.

- You want your partner to help out more at home. Are they more likely to hear what you are asking for if

a) you have just had a serious argument
b) you have just done something thoughtful for them?

No prizes for knowing that the answer is b.

The ability to assess and use your leverage is vital and some of the things that increase or decrease your leverage are shown in the table below.[51]

You have MORE leverage relative to someone else if you...	You have LESS leverage relative to someone else if you...
• Have a higher position	• Have a lower position
• Have more occupational status	• Have less occupational status
• Have something the other person needs	• Do not have anything the other person needs
• Are the sole provider of a resource	• Have strong competition
• Have influence with people in authority	• Do not know people in authority
• Have abilities that are hard to replace	• Have easily replaceable abilities
• Have other ways to get your needs met	• Are dependent on the other person

51 McIntyre, 2005.

You have MORE leverage relative to someone else if you...	You have LESS leverage relative to someone else if you...
• Have a good reputation or track record	• Have a poor reputation or no track record
• Have a positive relationship with the other person	• Have a poor relationship with the other person
• Have less emotional attachment to the issue at hand	• Have a greater emotional attachment to the issue at hand

The last quality in the table above really made me stop and think when I first read it. I have always prided myself on being passionate about and committed to my work, and I have only ever seen this as a source of strength. Dr McIntyre convinced me otherwise when she pointed out the following:

"Although feeling passionate about your job is a plus, too much passion can be dysfunctional. Dedication to your work may make you credible and persuasive, but those who are too emotionally invested in their jobs can become defensive and inflexible. People who overreact to critiques or constructive suggestions tend to be difficult to work with, so the ability to disengage emotions and view issues objectively can increase your influence. When you develop a reputation as an unbiased and thoughtful observer, others are more likely to seek you out for consultation. As more people consult you, your leverage will increase."[52]

---

52   McIntyre, 2005.

Exercise: How much leverage do you have? [53]

Leverage boosters	Definitely	Somewhat	Not really
Results: I produce results that provide a clear benefit to my organisation	3	2	1
Knowledge: I possess knowledge that is quite useful to my organisation	3	2	1
Attitude: I am viewed by almost everyone as helpful and cooperative	3	2	1
Empathy: People often come to me for help with their problems or concerns	3	2	1
Networks: I know many people throughout my organisation	3	2	1
Inclusion: I typically try to include other people in my decisions or projects	3	2	1
Detachment: I am known as someone who can view situations objectively	3	2	1
Total score:			

Score of 18 – 21: You probably possess a great deal of leverage. I only say "probably" because we must always be open to blind spots in how we are truly showing up. If your self-assessment is accurate, well done! With this amount of leverage, you should be able to get a lot done.

---

53   McIntyre, 2005.

Score of 11 – 17: You certainly have opportunities to increase your leverage if you want to.

Score less than 10: You definitely have some work to do.

If your score is lower than you would like it to be, identify the categories where you could improve. What specific steps could you take to increase your leverage in these areas? What could you do differently, either in terms of what you are doing at work and/or how you are interacting with people at work?

Keeping things Win/Win

Stephen Covey's work on the Seven Habits of Highly Effective People has many insights that apply to political intelligence. His fifth habit, "Seek first to understand and then be understood" lies at the heart of all the interpersonal influence skills discussed thus far while his fourth habit, "Keep things Win/Win" is crucial to improving your social awareness and in turn, your political intelligence and effectiveness. He is quite right when he says that keeping things Win/Win (and wanting to do so) is far more than just a technique. It's fundamentally about how you see the world and how you choose to interact with others in discussions, debates or formal negotiations.

- Win – this is about you winning at all costs, irrespective of what happens to other people. They may be okay after engaging with you. They may not. It doesn't matter as long as you win and come out on top.

- Win/Lose – this is about you winning and needing others to come out worse as a result.

- Lose/Win – this happens when you just give in to others in order to keep the peace, or to stop things getting worse. Ironically, the anger and resentment you feel as a result can end up doing even more damage to the relationship than upfront frankness would have done.

- Lose/Lose – this is the classic example of 'cutting off your nose to spite your face'. The example Covey gives is a divorce, where a judge orders the husband to sell his assets and give half the proceeds to his wife. He complies by selling his car that is worth $10 000 for only $50 and giving $25 to his ex-wife.

- Win/Win or No Deal – this often happens when people are starting out in a business or a partnership where it is agreed that if both parties can't benefit, then each will walk away with no hard feelings.

- Win/Win – in these scenarios, as Covey says so beautifully, you need to balance "courage (your win) *and* consideration (the other person's win)". If it is all about courage, such that consideration doesn't even feature, then you are thinking Win/Lose. If on the other hand, it is all about the other person and you take a back seat, then you are back to a Lose/Win situation.[54]

None of us wants to feel that we lost in a situation – either because another person didn't show us enough consideration or because we didn't have enough courage to stand up for ourselves. The beauty in trying to find Win/Win solutions is that very often possibilities you wouldn't have otherwise noticed, appear. This lies at the heart of successful negotiations, but you don't have to be a professional negotiator to try to look for continuous opportunities for Win/Win in your interactions and relationships with other people.

One of the most valuable pieces of advice I ever received was: "If you have a choice between being effective and being right, choose being effective."

Effectiveness comes from building your relationship with someone else, rather than walking all over it. It comes from seeing what else might be

---

54   Covey, 2004.

possible if you put your heads together, rather than assuming your way is the only answer. In a nutshell, it comes from wanting as far as possible, to keep things Win/Win.

Managing the perceptions others have of you

When we think of a 'brand' we mistakenly tend to think of corporate identity: the logo, colours, 'look and feel' of a company or organisation. In fact, a brand is nothing more than a promise – one which is captured to some degree in the corporate identity, but which is far more than a symbol. It is about being clear on what people can expect of you when they deal with you and then consistently delivering on those expectations at every opportunity.

Brands apply to individuals just as much as they apply to organisations. Tom Peters pointed this out 20 years ago in an article that has since become a classic:

"Regardless of age, regardless of position, regardless of the business we happen to be in, all of us need to understand the importance of branding. We are CEOs of our own companies: Me Inc. To be in business today, our most important job is to

be head marketer for the
brand called You. It's that
simple — and that hard.
And that inescapable."[55]

To start thinking about yourself as a brand, ask yourself the question that all brand managers of companies have to ask and answer continuously: What do I do that makes me valuable to have around? Try to answer this in 15 words or less. Once you've come up with the answer, re-read it a few times. Does what you have put down excite you? Inspire you? Would it excite or inspire anyone else, like a manager, or a client, or a colleague, or a prospective employer? If not, it's time to do some work and give some real thought to what you want your brand to be and what you want it to stand for.

Exercise: The Brand called You

- Start by thinking about what makes you different and distinctive from other people you work with:

    o   What have you done recently to make yourself stand out or be noticed?

    o   What would people who work with you say is your biggest strength and most worthwhile quality?

- When companies think about their brand and how it compares to others, e.g. Coke vs Pepsi, Mercedes vs BMW, Apple vs Samsung, the usual approach is feature-benefit: "Every feature they offer in their product or service yields an identifiable and distinguishable benefit for their customer or client."

    o   What is your brand "feature-benefit"?

        □   Maybe you deliver what you say you will, on time, every time?

---

55   Peters, 1997.

- □ Perhaps you can be counted on to always bring discretionary energy to your job in such a way that you don't just deliver what is expected, but go far beyond that?
- □ Do you help your team see opportunities and imagine possibilities in ways that no-one else can?
- □ What else?

- Now forget about your job title, your job description, your KPIs, your place on the organogram. Forget about all of that and ask yourself instead: "What do I do that adds remarkable, measurable, distinguished, distinctive value? What do I do that I am most proud of? (Because) if you're going to be a brand, you've got to become relentlessly focused on what you do that adds value, that you're proud of, and most importantly, that you can shamelessly take credit for."[56]

- Once you've done all of that, the last and most important question to ask yourself in defining your brand is: "What do I want to be famous for?" Does that sound laughable? An impossible stretch? Nonsense! You have only one life. If you are not excited and inspired about what you want to do with it and for others while you have it, why are you getting up every morning?

- Once you have decided this, you need to start living it, and living it visibly. There is an almost infinite number of ways you can do this. Volunteer for extra projects in your department. Post articles on LinkedIn. Have your brand at the back of your mind every time you engage with someone, go to a meeting, give a presentation, send an email or answer an email. What do you want people to think, or know, or feel about you, and are you projecting that in big ways and small, in every interaction you have?

- The biggest success for any branding campaign – be it the Brand called You, or any company – is 'word of mouth.' "Your network of friends, colleagues, clients, and customers is the most important marketing vehicle you've got; what they say about you and your contributions is what the market will ultimately gauge as the value of your brand. So the big trick to building your brand is to find ways to nurture your network of colleagues – consciously."[57]

---

56   Peters, 1997.

57   Peters, 1997.

- You need to use the power that you have to build your brand and in turn, use your brand to build your power. I spoke about personal and political power in Chapter 3. When it comes to personal branding, the power you need to harness and continuously build is reputational power. This is the power that comes from people knowing that you are good at what you do so that they want to be around that power, harness it and/or benefit from it. Power continues to be important when it comes to your own personal brand, so attaining it and using it responsibly is vital. You can do this in all kind of ways – it does not have to be a case of your ego entering the room two minutes before you do. Largely, it is about perception. People see you in many ways, much of which is determined by how much you believe in, live and project your brand.

- Finally, you need to find ways to ask for regular feedback on how you are doing. Honest, helpful feedback is a blessing. Honest, helpful, negative feedback is even better, because it is so rare that people show the courage and the kindness to provide negative, 'constructive' feedback. When you receive feedback about your performance, your value, or your contributions, take a deep breath and use it to 'sharpen your saw' and refine what you are putting out there.

All of this can be summed up in the idea that politically, "invisible contributions have no value". If what you are doing is known only to yourself, or visible only to one or two colleagues, then you are probably missing out on important opportunities to build your brand in ways that count. I am not saying that you need to boast about yourself at every opportunity and turn into the kind of self-centred person that no-one can stand to be around. That is clearly an extreme to be avoided. Equally so though, the opposite extreme of quietly getting on with things in the background, waiting to be acknowledged and rewarded, is one that doesn't do you or your career any favours.

There is a particular relevance in all of this for women. There is considerable, ongoing research that shows that when it comes to being promoted or appointed, both male and female managers tend to appoint men based on their potential, while women tend to be promoted on their actual, proven track record.[58] [59] This gender distinction is a whole separate and important discussion, but it amplifies the point that what you have done needs to be known to count in your favour – personally, professionally and politically.

Development Activities identified by CCL[60]

Political Skill	Development Activities	Why Is This Important?
Social Awareness	• Focus on understanding what motivates the people with whom you work. Identify the incentives and agendas that are driving the behaviours. • When attempting to influence or persuade others, show them how your proposed idea actually helps them achieve their goals and agendas. • Pay attention to the language others use as well as their body language. Observe physical behaviours such as eye contact and gestures as clues to a person's feelings and motives. • Tailor your interactions with others based on your analysis of their motives. Flex and adjust your style to meet the needs of others.	Any good navigator must understand the terrain he or she is travelling. The same hold true when utilising the practice of social awareness. Whether it is entering a meeting or speaking to someone one-on-one, there are many social cues that give you an idea of how people are feeling, their level of engagement and interest, and their intentions. Researchers have found that up to 93% of the meaning conveyed when communicating is nonverbal, which means there is a lot of information available to a leader in social interactions beyond what is actually said.[61]

---

58   Sandberg, 2013.

59   Player, Randsley de Moura, Leite, Abrams & Tresh, 2019.

60   Braddy & Campbell, 2014.

61   Gentry & Kuhnert, 2007.

Political Skill	Development Activities	Why Is This Important?
Social Awareness (Continued)	• If you're planning to have one-on-one meetings with others, develop some talking points to help you engage others and make them feel comfortable. • Spend some time thinking about and planning how to make a positive impression on others, but remember to still be genuine.	Researchers at MIT's Human Dynamics Laboratory have found that *how* teams communicate is much more important to high performance than *what* is said.[62]

Networking

Networking is really just about having mutually beneficial relationships with a wide range of diverse people. And one of the most powerful, and true, things I've ever heard is: "Some of the most important decisions of your career are going to be taken when you are not in the room. So who is in the room on your behalf?" People visibly do a double-take when I say this, because it is quite a big realisation for them to consider and understand – generally for the first time.

Some people are not big fans of networking at all, because they think they are too shy or that they don't know how to do it. Others take a very cynical view of the whole concept of networking, rolling their eyes and saying that "there is only a one-letter difference between networking and not working… "[63] Still others think that it is an unnecessary distraction from their "real" work and one that they can't afford to waste time on. And then there are those who think that 'networking' only happens at formal events that are labelled as such and if you don't have the time, inclination or interest to attend them and hand out business cards, then you cannot network.

---

62 Pentland, 2013.

63 Kaiser, Chamorro-Premuzic & Lusk, 2017.

I agree completely with the idea that networking is, in fact, the "number one unwritten rule of success in business."[64] I have found this to be absolutely true in my own career, one where I have not looked for a role since my first one. All the roles that I have held have been offered to me by people who knew me or knew of me. Bear in mind that the positions I have held haven't just seen me move within an industry, doing more of the same kind of work, only at different companies. Instead, I have changed industries completely – from the private sector to the public sector, from civil society to my own business, from corporate to consulting, from South Africa to companies around the world.

At the same time, all of my roles have seen me be the first person in a newly created position. So I was the first CEO of the Businesswomen's Association; then the first CEO of NOAH (Nurturing Orphans of AIDS for Humanity); the first Head of External Strategy at the South African Reserve Bank, and more. I say this not to boast but to emphasise the important point that, while I have certain skills, it is the network of people who know about my skills that affords me the opportunities to apply them. I could have had all the skills in the world, but never any chance to apply them without my network working for me.

The same is true now, with my own business. All the work that I do and am grateful to have has come to me from my networks. I have also given work to others though, and this is the critical thing to remember about networking – it must be mutually beneficial. If it only goes one way, such that you are the one who is always taking, it is not networking – it is using people. To be in a mutually beneficial network, you need to give and pay things forward.

And you do *not* need to play golf, or go mountain biking! Nine times out of ten, someone in a lecture will bring this up on the subject of networking. I have to say that the idea that all networking happens on a golf course really annoys me, because underlying this observation is the assumption that not having a good network is something that is outside of a person's control, simply because they don't play a particular sport. I do not play golf (unless you count putt-putt with my nieces and nephews?) and my network is extensive. Yes, I can see from friends and colleagues who do play the game that many conversations inevitably happen on a golf course. I should

64   Krawcheck, 2016.

hope so, taking into account the amount of time spent walking along and playing the course together. But it is not the only way and the only place where networking happens. Thinking that it is lazy, unimaginative and quite frankly, a cop-out.

There are all manner of other ways that people who want to network, can – WhatsApp groups, LinkedIn, face-to-face events, coffee conversations, book clubs, parties... And you can do so whether you are an off-the-chart extrovert, or someone who is much quieter or introverted. Whatever your personality type and however you choose to network, you will put the time, trouble and effort into doing so only if you recognise how important it is. One way or another, networking really just requires that you look up from what you think is your 'real work' and put some time and effort into cultivating relationships with new colleagues and acquaintances, perhaps in different lines of work. Given that politics are about relationships, rather than being a distraction, relationships are a currency that you need to build on and invest in if you want to build your political capital.

It is absolutely true that "those who loudly complain that 'it's just who you know' are usually the ones who never take the initiative to get to know anyone."[65]

---

65   McIntyre, 2005.

Exercise: Audit your network and networking style[66]

Do a quick audit of your network by asking yourself the following questions:

• I have a broad and extensive network of people across levels, functions, demographics in the organisation and outside of it	My network shows signs of: • **Clustering**, i.e. everyone – or almost everyone in it – is of the same demographic (white, middle-aged women etc.) and/or • **Layering,** i.e. is concentrated only at a particular level so that it doesn't extend up or down levels and/or • **Having occupational tunnel vision, i.e.** consists mainly of people in my own department or particular function
• I have identified the people I need to know to achieve what I want to	• I have no idea who could or should be helping me achieve what I need to
• I actively look for opportunities to interact with others	• I spend most of my day at my desk, doing my work or by myself
• I push myself outside of my comfort zone to try new things or meet different people	• I tend to prefer sticking to people who are like me
• I try to find things that I have in common with other people and then build conversations on these common interests	• I only ever speak to people about work matters
• I try to help others where I can	• If something is not in my job description, I don't do it
• I allow myself to be helped by others where and when I need it	• I'm not a big believer in asking others for help. Even if I did want to ask them for help, I wouldn't know who to turn to

---

66   McIntyre, 2005.

If your answers tend to be in the left column, you are on the right track to building up a wide and useful network. If your answers were much more in the right column, then you need to look at what you can do to improve your network and your networking skills.

Development Activities identified by CCL[67]

Political Skill	Development Activities	Why Is This Important?
Networking	• Become aware of your existing network and to whom you tend to go for advice information, and resources. Determine whether your network is too restrictive. • Expand your network by building new relationships with others who may be outside of your group, team, or function. • Focus on building a diverse network, not just a large network. A diverse network provides access to different and unique viewpoints, resources, and opportunities. • Avoid building connections only when you need something. Rather, build relationships with others for the right reasons (e.g., you have genuine interest in them).	With the complexity leaders face, it simply is not possible for a single person to have the necessary skills, knowledge, and abilities to solve all problems and always make wise decisions. Effective leaders build and use their networks to tap into the resources, knowledge, and skills of others in order to handle complex challenges. Research on networks has found that for leaders, bigger does not mean better. Instead, effective leaders build targeted and diverse networks that extend their current knowledge and abilities. These leaders know when and where to build their networks as well as when to decrease connectivity with individuals.[68]

---

67   Braddy & Campbell, 2014.

68   Cross & Thomas, 2008.

Political Skill	Development Activities	Why Is This Important?
Networking (Continued)	• Maintaining good relationships takes time and effort. You need to spend time with others, even when you don't need something from them. • Spend time with others when you can connect with them on a personal level (e.g., during lunch or after hours). • Make sure you are connected to both higher-level and lower-level people in your organisation. • Leverage your networks and connections to get things done and to secure valuable resources for your group. One way to get others to help you is by first helping them. This draws on the principle of reciprocity.	One of the common network traps leaders fall into is insularity. An insular network can develop when leaders are primarily connecting with like-minded individuals who share very similar perspectives. Having an insular network can mean the leader is limiting his or her access to new ideas and different insights.[69]

Sincerity

Ferris's original work found that it wasn't sincerity itself that was the political skill, but rather the *appearance* of sincerity because (as he quite cynically observed) "how honest you think you are is far less important than how honest other people think you are."[70] As such, the research called the practice "Apparent Sincerity". I imagine we can all think of many examples of people showing up like this. When doing their research though, the CCL

---

69 Willburn & Campbell, 2012.

70 Kaiser, Chamorro-Premuzic & Lusk, 2017.

changed this practice to "sincerity" because they agreed this was more accurate in terms of what was really going when politically smart people practised politics to their advantage. I think both have a valid point, but for the purposes of consistency, I will talk about "Sincerity".[71]

Apologising – properly – when it is called for

There are many actions and words that demonstrate sincerity, but one of the most vital that I have seen is the ability to know when to apologise and how.

It often comes as a surprise to people that there is power, strength and opportunity in an apology. Yet, there most certainly is, precisely because sincere apologies are so difficult to offer and therefore so rare. Admitting we are wrong can be difficult to do and very humbling. Taking that realisation a step further by actually apologising for what we have said or done, is even more difficult. How much more tempting to just sweep it under the carpet, pretend it never happened and hope, or expect, the other person to just 'get over it'?

There are many reasons for this. A common one is that we may think that whoever apologises is 'more guilty' or the 'loser' of the conflict. And yet, offering an apology, even when only a small part of the conflict was your responsibility is no bad thing. It allows you to get clear what you regret about what you did, but also confirms your boundaries. As such, it's no surprise that numerous stories have been shared in my lectures of how an unexpected apology, particularly from a manager or someone more senior, has done an enormous amount towards building respect and repairing relationships that had been damaged by an action that was unfair.

No doubt you can think of examples of your own where this has been true. In those instances, it was not only the fact of the apology but its sincerity that made all the difference. A dismissive or insincere apology can actually do more harm than good. Saying something glib and vague like "I'm sorry if what I did somehow offended you" is basically sending a message that someone's hurt feelings are their own fault and have nothing to do with you.

---

71   Braddy & Campbell, 2014.

Equally, just saying the words "I'm sorry" is not enough. What are you sorry *for*? *Why* was it hurtful or wrong? As a delegate once said very firmly and unequivocally to all of us during a lecture I was giving: "If my husband doesn't know *what* he's apologising for, I don't want to hear it!"

So when is it a good time to apologise? Well, two good (and obvious) places to start are when you've made a mistake, or you have hurt someone else. Apologising in these cases is not only for the sake of the person you've 'wronged' but also about making yourself feel better. Guilt and regret are terrible feelings to carry around and they become corrosive if you cannot at least try to mitigate them by apologising to those who were harmed by what you did. "Not apologising when you are wrong can be damaging to your personal and professional relationships. It can also lead to rumination, anger, resentment, and hostility that may only grow over time."[72]

I heard a radio interview years ago with a woman who was a nursery school teacher. She spoke about the technique they used for teaching the young children in their care how to apologise sincerely. Quite frankly, I think it's a technique all of us would benefit from learning – and applying.

1. I am sorry for… (what you did – or didn't do – that you regret)

2. It was wrong because … (taking responsibility for what you did)

3. I wish I could… (showing that you regret what you did so that the person knows that you actually care about what you did and about the impact that it had on them)

4. In future, I will… (making a commitment to the other person so they can hold you accountable to do something different in future, either in terms of how you will behave, or the boundaries of your relationship, etc.)

5. Is there anything I can do to make it better now?

---

72   Scott, 2020.

Development Activities identified by CCL[73]

Political Skill	Development Activities	Why Is This Important?
Sincerity	• Become aware of whether others perceive you to be authentic and genuine. • Make sure to follow through on your commitments in order to build trusting relationships. • Be purposeful and clear in how you compliment or reward others. In other words, be genuine. • Be transparent in communicating with others to avoid the appearance of withholding information. • Treat all your subordinates equally and fairly. Avoid creating the perception of showing favouritism. • Don't rush trust; it takes a long time to build and only a short time to lose. • Don't be afraid to show your vulnerability to others. • Allow others to see you express a range of natural emotions. It is okay to let others see you when you are upset, frustrated, or disappointed.	Building trusting relationships is critical to effectively leading others. Trust is built over time and through multiple interactions, which makes displaying sincerity critical. Research from the Reina Trust Building Institute has identified three ways that leaders build trust: (1) by doing what you say you will do; (2) by displaying a willingness to share information, tell the truth, and admit mistakes; and (3) by displaying confidence in others' abilities to perform and make decisions. Leaders who display trust in these ways will find that trust is reciprocal – the more they give, the more trust they receive in return from others.[74]

---

73 Braddy & Campbell, 2014.

74 Reina and Reina, 2006.

In conclusion

So there you have them. Four practices, with a few elements of each, that are the hallmark of people who have good political intelligence and who use it to their benefit. During one of my lectures, we were discussing some of these elements and qualities. I asked the group if there was anything that they found particularly interesting or surprising about what I had covered. A woman at the back of the room put up her hand and, with a shocked expression on her face, said loudly, "Yes! It's a lot of work!"

She was absolutely right. It *is* a lot of work to apply yourself to things that seem to be over and above what you think is your actual work – delivering projects, trying to get even a semblance of control over your email inbox, hoping that after a day of meetings you actually have the time to accomplish all the things that the meetings added to your already long 'to-do' list. Yet, this *is* your work, if you are going to build the power, relationships and reputation that will allow you to accomplish what you want to, successfully. We so often think in binary, 'either-or' terms, but with office politics and career success, it is always a 'both-and'.

Proficiency in politics also depends on what motivates you when it comes to your career and your life. I have a very impressive friend and ex-colleague whose family was in exile for most of her childhood. As such, she only came to South Africa for the first time as a young adult, after having lived a very nomadic life across Africa and Canada. Twenty years later, she is an extremely successful business owner, a fire-cracker when it comes to raising money for her favourite charities and a very devoted and hands-on parent. I remember asking her once how she managed to achieve so much and do so with such effortless grace. Her reply? "I see all the things on my to-do list as things that my mother never got the chance to do. Knowing that, fires me up to do as much as I possibly can with every day of my life."

So are these things simple? On many levels, yes.

Are they easy? Certainly not.

Are they critical to your career success? Without a doubt.

CHAPTER 5

A Few Political Mistakes You Really Should Avoid

"In war you can only be killed once. In politics, you can be killed many times."

–Winston Churchill

Mistakes in life are inevitable. Many times, they are also the only way that we truly learn what we need to – in life, in love and at work. That said, this section is about trying to help you avoid some unnecessary and painful mistakes.

I have learnt an enormous amount from the mistakes I have made, including what I really want, and don't want; who I want to be, and who I definitely do *not* want to be. But my mistakes were painful and the lessons difficult. With hindsight, more than a few of them were also entirely unnecessary. If I had known the things I know now, I could well have done all manner of things better and differently.

I saw some important situations as Win/Lose, Either/Or, Right/Wrong battles to be fought and won. If I had seen them instead as simply different perspectives, I could have been much more effective for myself and my teams. That is not to say that there aren't many things that I have done well in my career and that I am justifiably proud of. But those are for another book. This section is about trying to save you some of the pain that others and I have gone through.

Mistake #1: Becoming The Problem

The moment you start to become "The Problem", things will become extremely unpleasant very quickly. If I had read the following passage at one particular point in my career, I would have had warning signs flashing at me from every direction, telling me I was heading for trouble. Serious trouble.

"Sociologists and marketers describe a phenomenon known as the tipping point. A tipping point occurs when for example, a disease unexpectedly begins to spread like wildfire, becoming an epidemic, or a new product suddenly catches on all over the country, quickly selling out in every store. I often witness this 'tipping' phenomenon when managers are grappling with difficult employee situations. The decision to demote or fire someone is seldom made suddenly. But the point at which such drastic action becomes an option – the tipping point – is when the person begins to be seen as The Problem. Once someone is tagged with that label, a marked shift occurs in the manager's thinking: instead of considering how to either coach or cope with the employee, the manager is now starting to fantasise about how pleasant life would be if this bothersome person were gone and to wonder how many 'last chances' should be provided before the axe falls."[75]

When I have managed people who became The Problem, I have had these fantasies and frustrations. Eventually, after trying everything, I have been left with no choice but to move them on. As difficult as it has been to do this, it is certainly less difficult and damaging than keeping Problems around. A colleague of mine said it well, "Niven, if you can't change the people, change the people." Of course, this doesn't mean arbitrarily and on a whim getting rid of people. Far from it! Not only is that shirking your responsibility as a leader, but it is also really difficult to do, legally. As such, the onus is always on you as a manager to do everything you can and *should*, to support and help someone who is showing up as The Problem. But if and when you have done all that you can (and more) and the person's behaviour is still not improving or changing? Well, then it's time to "change the people".

There are many ways that we can become The Problem, but they all boil down to behaving in any way that takes up a disproportionate amount of a

---

75   McIntyre, 2005.

manager's time, attention and energy. If you are doing this, then you need to stop and think hard about where it is going to get you. One of the most common reasons for people becoming The Problem is that they let their emotions get the better of them. They see something as unfair and are not able, or willing, to get over it and get on with things.

The hard but inescapable reality is that things are never going to be fair. So as long as you do not have to deal with toxic or criminal-type behaviour, my only advice is to do exactly that – get over it and move on. Ask for help if you must – see a coach, seek the advice of friends you trust, or speak to a mentor. But stewing over things that are not going to change and telling yourself and anyone who will listen how hard done by you are, is a sure-fire road to political disaster and will not get you anywhere, other than in a deeper hole than the one you might already be in.

Self-assessment: How good are you at self-management?[76]

	Almost always	Often	Seldom	Almost never
1. I am always able to view my actions with the eye of an outside observer	4	3	2	1
2. I am often surprised by the way others view my behaviour	1	2	3	4
3. I tend to act without thinking	1	2	3	4
4. I am good at anticipating how people will react in different situations	4	3	2	1
5. I am able to keep myself from saying things that might be unwise	4	3	2	1
6. I believe in "doing what comes naturally" so that I can really be myself	1	2	3	4

---

76   McIntyre, 2005.

	Almost always	Often	Seldom	Almost never
7. I stop myself from doing things that could have negative consequences	4	3	2	1
8. I often regret the actions I have taken	1	2	3	4
9. I say things to others without considering how they may react	1	2	3	4
10. I find it hard to stop myself from doing things that I really want to do	1	2	3	4
11. I am consciously aware of my actions and reactions around others	4	3	2	1
12. I have tried to develop behaviours that are outside of my comfort zone	4	3	2	1
13. I tend to do things that are against my better judgement	1	2	3	4
14. I make conscious choices about what I say and do with others	4	3	2	1

Count the number of 4, 3, 2 and 1 scores that you gave yourself.

Higher Self Management Skills		Lower Self Management Skills	
Total 4's	Total 3's	Total 2's	Total 1's

The more scores you have on the left side of the chart, the better your self-management skills appear to be. The more scores on the right side, the more problems you may encounter in this area.

Mistake #2: Getting the leverage equation wrong

I spoke a lot in Chapter 4 about the concept of leverage. It is an important one to grasp and get comfortable with. One of the biggest political mistakes we can make in our careers is to get the leverage equation wrong, either by under- or overestimating it.

Underestimating your leverage

A common mistake, and one of my first, was underestimating my leverage with a company when it came to salary negotiations. Many of us have been asked, or have asked, the same question as the interviewing manager asked me: what my salary had been in my previous position. We all see it as a normal procedure; one that is perfectly reasonable and legitimate. That's certainly how I saw it, and so I duly told her what my salary had been. We then used that information as a basis for discussions and finalisation of what my salary would be in the position this organisation was offering me.

With hindsight, I realised that I should never have shared my previous salary information. It was irrelevant, given that it was for another job, with different responsibilities and a different mandate, at an entirely different organisation. All that was relevant was where the salary for this position had been benchmarked and going from that benchmark to finalise my salary. Instead, by setting a benchmark that was much lower than had been budgeted for, I did myself a significant financial disservice – with little argument from my new manager, of course.

Realising the knock I took on the salary I could have asked for, I resolved not to have this kind of conversation again. If I ever have a delegate from Human Resources (HR) or Human Capital (HC) in my lectures and this story comes up in discussion, I just know to expect all kinds of reasons as to why examining current payslips is an inevitable part of the governance process for bringing new hires on board. I completely disagree.

Another example that comes to mind is from one of my course delegates. She phoned me up a few weeks after the session and asked if we could meet for coffee. We duly did and had a long and interesting conversation about her current role and some of the challenges she was experiencing in it. By a strange coincidence, I happened to have done some strategy work for the company and so I knew the Exco members that she reported in to. After she finished telling me everything, I told her that she was entirely underestimating and underusing her leverage.

This delegate was technically very good at her job and she had been approached to fill the position. That gave her some definite leverage – the company wanted her for all that she could bring from a skills point of view. Over and above that, I reminded her that she was also the only woman and the only black person in her management layer and she was being groomed to take over a role in Exco one day; an Exco that was entirely white and male. This Exco was really committed to diversity and wanted to have her be part of changing the complexion and nature of the leadership of the company. These factors also gave her leverage.

Despite this leverage, she was spending a huge amount of time and energy trying to fix an untenable situation, rather than using these sources of leverage to get the Exco to take the action they should have years before to resolve it. She had power, but she didn't want to use it and so doing, was losing the opportunity to make things substantially better for herself, her team and ultimately the organisation.

Overestimating your leverage

I have also overestimated my leverage. One time in particular stands out. I was approached about a project by people who were very excited to have my abilities and expertise on board. After numerous discussions, I was delighted to take on the challenge and really looked forward to being part of work that would bring about changes that everyone agreed were long overdue and critical to the success of the organisation concerned.

Things went wonderfully at first but after about a year, it became increasingly apparent that the people who had brought me on board and I had very different ways of seeing things. The mandate that I had been given (which had convinced me to take on the work in the first place), was nowhere to be seen in practice, because the people with power were, in reality, very invested in the status quo remaining exactly the same. It may not have been good for the organisation and for thousands of people, but it was certainly good for them. As such, they were going to defend their turf with everything they had, not least because this was the only place they had worked and therefore, the only company they've ever known and been known in.

In assessing the situation, I thought that I had achieved enough in the role to give me professional leverage and that I had good enough relationships with the power players to give me personal leverage to speak about my concerns and propose some changes. In fact, I had completely overestimated my leverage. All of a sudden the work that I was doing, and my role in it came to a complete halt. It was dressed up very diplomatically and graciously as a decision to "roll things into business as usual" but my engagement there was summarily over. While I was truly delighted to be out of there, it was much *less* delightful to have a decision made about and for me, rather than having made it myself. And it was all because I got the leverage equation wrong.

Mistake #3: Being one person's person

Given that politics are all about the influence you have through building effective relationships with the right people, networks clearly matter. Having well-placed and supportive contacts, mentors and sponsors is always going to be a vital part of your success. That said, you can make mistakes when it comes to networking.

> One of the key mistakes you can make is to become "one person's person."

In a nutshell, this is where you become so aligned to one person that your reputation, success and the perceptions that others have of you are defined largely, if not exclusively, by this single relationship. This is all fine and well when your person is in favour and you benefit from their power and standing. It becomes a lot less fine if your person leaves or the political landscape shifts and your person suddenly loses favour and power.

I made this mistake once in my career and it taught me a lot. I have been fortunate to work with, and for, some truly impressive people that I will always admire and respect. This particular leader is at the top of my list. In the time that I worked for him, I was able to achieve an enormous amount. Together, we made quite a powerful force; one which achieved significant milestones for the organisation and unleashed a real sense of possibility for its people. I am still proud of that time and what we made happen.

On reflection, there is however one thing that I can I fault this extraordinary man on; his reaction when I came to him for help before the start of a particularly difficult initiative. Thinking about all that lay ahead and all the hurdles that needed to be navigated, I said that I needed him to "please handle the politics with Exco" because I didn't have the time or the appetite for it. I asked him to take care of it, so that I could free up my time and energy to focus on what we needed to deliver. He agreed and at the time, I was grateful and relieved that he did exactly what I had asked him to do, namely watch my back and clear my way. As he fought all kinds of battles on my behalf, many of which I never even knew about, I was saved the 'hassle' of having to get Exco on my side, knowing that he was doing it and that I just had to push ahead with the task at hand.

It's only in hindsight that I understood the mistake he and I had both made. In seeking to support me as he always unfailingly did, he allowed me to duck out of something that I should have made a key responsibility, namely to do the hard work of getting Exco on my side. Given the dynamics of this team, I would have struggled to get their support by myself. I would have needed his support and advice to keep them on our side and to address their concerns continuously. That said, we could – and should – have done this together and built up a real coalition with the committee. Instead, because I was too busy 'getting on with things' and leaving him to 'deal with the politics', I had no relationship with Exco members, other than through him. This meant I was completely exposed when things changed and he moved from his position to a horizontal role in the company.

All of a sudden, I was without his direct support to continue with the work that we had started. I had fallen into the trap of becoming 'one person's person' and while being 'his person' was enormously effective for as long as he could have my back, it was anything but helpful when things changed and he could no longer pave the way for me.

Do not make the same mistake. As tempting as it is to work only with the people you like and to assume that they will always be there for you, the reality is that things change. Always and inevitably. If you want to be politically smart, you need to build a range of alliances and relationships, fully aware that doing so is a critical part of your work, rather than a distraction from it.

Mistake #4: Failing to (even try to) convert adversaries to allies

Since your political capital and leverage depends on the number and nature of your relationships at work, then obviously the more adversaries you have, the more exposed you are politically. You take a risk every time you can't be bothered to understand why someone is an adversary, i.e. what conditions of theirs are not being met so that they are not on your side. Dale Carnegie said it really well years ago:

"Ultimately, people do things not for our reasons but for their reasons."

So what *are* their reasons? What matters to *them*? Finding this out and *wanting* to find it out can make all the difference. By the same token, not doing so can really come back to bite you.

Mistake #5: Making unnecessary adversaries or foes

Any time you make an unnecessary adversary, or worse, a foe, you are really setting yourself up for all kinds of difficulty. Sometimes it's not even about the number of foes or adversaries we make – just one wrong adversary can make things enormously difficult and stressful for us. Once again, I have made this mistake and I still remember the intense frustration of the experience.

In this case, I made an adversary of the Chief Whisperer. I don't know where I first heard this term. I have Googled it several times, but can find no reference and so I cannot give credit where credit is due. As soon as I read it though, I knew what it meant. Any time I mention it in lectures, everyone else *also* knows exactly what it means.

The Chief Whisperer exists in every organisation, department or team. They do not confront or block you obviously and as such, it is easy to underestimate what they are capable of if they are not on your side. Being a Chief Whisperer is not about formal or obvious power. The one that I came up against was, in fact, someone in a position junior to mine. His power didn't come from his formal position, but from the fact that he had been around for years and had long-standing and *very* close friendships with the power players I reported in to.

Personal histories that go back years, carry tremendous weight and what I was seeing on the surface was not what was going on, or being discussed, behind the scenes. I was the newcomer, who didn't understand 'how we do things around here'. He was the person who had only ever done great things in the minds of the power players, even if not in the reality of my experience or the stories of many others who had seen him fail and be rescued and praised, regardless. The more he and I butted heads about who should be doing what, the more his whispering to my line manager gained pace and the more my relationship with both of them deteriorated.

The reality is that for all kinds of reasons, Chief Whisperers have the ear of people in power and they can, and will, use that power to say all manner of things about you; things that you will probably never know, never hear about and therefore never be able to counter. Instead, what you will slowly start to see is that perceptions of you are shifting, that you are finding it increasingly difficult to get things done and that you are being excluded.

Mistake #6: Not accepting or understanding the reality of organisations

It bears repeating (because it is so important to understand but so difficult to accept) that in reality, life is not 'fair'. Organisations are not democracies.

They are about power and hierarchy, and people with the most power win. Your boss or manager has significant power over your career, whether you like it or not. Ignoring these facts can result in you showing up in a way that does not serve you politically.

Years ago, I was going through a difficult time at work. I went to my coach, a wise and wonderful woman, and spluttered out all my frustrations and concerns. Having heard all my moaning, she just looked at me very calmly and said: "Niven, you are ignoring the reality of the situation. And the reality is that you are working for a large organisation. Large organisations do not change easily, if at all. And no matter what mandate you have to change it, you are not actually going to be able to achieve very much. This is not because you are not talented, resourceful, or good at your job. It is because it's the nature of the beast. If you keep ignoring this, or fighting against it, one of three things will happen. One, you will get resentful. Two, you will become resigned. Three, you will become self-righteous."

I didn't say anything for a good minute or two. I just looked at her, thinking long and hard about what she had said. Eventually, I took a deep breath and asked her: "And what if I become all three at once?!" After she told me this hard truth and I truly understood it, I started tempering my expectations and showing up very differently in how I engaged. This was quite difficult for me, because I think that I can make anything and everything better if I just try hard enough. Slowly but surely, the situation turned around, but I needed to hear and accept that difficult and uncomfortable reality before it did.

In conclusion

It is quite a vulnerable experience to share what I have, as they are stories of my own mistakes and egoism, failure and frustration. I find myself wanting to finish this chapter by telling you (and myself!) all the wonderful things that I've also done, to even out the scales a bit. I will resist that temptation though and instead, give you some closing advice from Jocelyn Davis:

"Keep friends close. Keep allies closer. Keep an open mind about adversaries. Keep foes to a minimum – and far away."[77]

Self-assessment: Warning signs of political trouble[78]

Having read about some of my mistakes, take a read through what Dr Marie McIntyre identifies as warning signs. If you spot any of these signals, you are very likely heading for a political cliff of one sort or another and you need to start acting differently. Fast.

Level 1: Something is not quite right

- You have been experiencing a growing uneasiness, with frequent angry thoughts about unfairness. (Sometimes people feel like a victim because they are actually about to become one.)

- You find yourself alone a lot. No one stops by your desk unless they have a specific purpose. You don't get invited to lunch, weddings, baby showers etc. You seem to have become a bit of a social outcast.

- Your boss ignores you, fails to notify you of meetings or to acknowledge you in meetings, neglects to give you information, or makes comments that you are requiring too much time and attention.

- Your boss has a Serious Talk with you about some aspect of your performance or personality. If your manager tends to avoid confrontation or be confrontation averse, this 'talk' may sound more like a chat than a reprimand. Consider your manager's style – anything out of the ordinary counts as a warning.

---

77 Davis, 2016.

78 McIntyre, 2005.

- A personal coach is hired to help you. The bad news is that you are seen as having some 'issues' that need to be addressed. The good news is that someone is still willing to invest in your future success. Companies seldom spend money on people they consider hopeless.

Level 2: The future looks questionable

- An important assignment or opportunity that would logically be yours is given to someone else. If that someone else has designs on your job or is a rival for your next promotion, you should be concerned.

- You are turned down for promotions more than once. The first time this happens, they may have just found a better applicant. But if it happens more than once then the pattern you are seeing is not a good one.

- You have a new boss and your leverage seems to be disappearing because you are not consulted as often or included in as many meetings as before. If you don't take some action, you are probably headed for that Serious Talk.

- Someone from HR initiates the Serious Talk. This is an indication that management has had some concerns about you for some time.

Level 3: A sudden career change may lie ahead

- Following a reorganisation, you find that you have fewer staff or your title, responsibilities or reporting level have changed. You were probably given a weak excuse for this change. If believing it makes you feel better, go ahead but recognise that any kind of reduction is a bad thing.

- Your boss's boss comes into the picture, reinforcing a Serious Talk that you have already had with someone else. This is not just a warning signal. It's a huge flashing neon sign.

- Rumours of retrenchments are going around, and people are starting to avoid you or look at you sadly. If these are HR people, start working on your CV.

Self-assessment: Are you a candidate for political suicide?[79]

Do you frequently feel angry or anxious at work?	YES	NO	MAYBE
If so, is your anger or anxiety obvious to other people?	YES	NO	MAYBE
Do you feel that you have been treated very unfairly at work?	YES	NO	MAYBE
Do you mentally review this unfair treatment on a regular basis?	YES	NO	MAYBE
Do you frequently talk about your unfair treatment with people at work?	YES	NO	MAYBE
Are you involved in a sexual or romantic relationship at work?	YES	NO	MAYBE
Do you focus exclusively on your own goals with little regard for others?	YES	NO	MAYBE
Would co-workers describe you as difficult to work with?	YES	NO	MAYBE
Have you felt resentful about a recent change at work?	YES	NO	MAYBE
Has this resentment caused you to exhibit annoying or disruptive behaviour?	YES	NO	MAYBE
Has a manager or HR person indicated that you need to make some changes?	YES	NO	MAYBE

If you have more than two or three 'yes' or 'maybe' answers then you could be heading for career trouble. Perhaps you are already right in the middle of it.

For any question where you answered 'yes' or 'maybe', you need to start considering your behaviour. To do so, you need to take a long hard look at

---

79   McIntyre, 2005.

your attitude and perspective. The fact that other people are treating you unfairly or behaving badly is irrelevant. You need to focus on yourself and what you are trying to achieve. In other words, what are the things that are within your control? If you want to keep your job, what do you need to do to hold onto it? If you don't necessarily want to stay in this position, what is your first step to move forward and find another one?

Self-assessment: Do you need political plastic surgery?[80]

If you have become your own greatest obstacle to success, then you need to start your political makeover. Take a good look at your own behaviour. What is causing others to conclude that you are a problem? What behaviours do you need to stop? What new behaviours do you need to start showing? Fill out the AMISH chart below.

Awareness: What am I doing that is creating a problem?	Motivation: Why is it important for me to change?	Identification: What are the specific harmful behaviours I need to stop?	Substitution: If I stop this behaviour, what helpful behaviour will I put in its place?	Habits: How will I know when my new behaviour has become a habit?

- Now that you have defined the behaviour you want to embody, identify the situations in which you need to use it. Think about the people or events that are most likely to trigger you. Mentally rehearse how you will handle both the people and the situation.

- Think about whether you need to have any discussions to start repairing perceptions. Do you need to tell anyone about your intention to make changes? If people from management or HR have had a Serious Talk with you, then I would definitely advise you to follow up with them, especially if you were initially dismissive of their feedback. The purpose of these conversations is to let them know you

---

80 McIntyre, 2005.

want to change your behaviour and describe what you intend to do differently. You must *not* get defensive, argue, complain or blame. If you don't have this type of self-control, then it's probably better not to have the discussion at all. Rather work on having your actions speak louder than your words.

- After a while, request some feedback to see how things are going. Follow-up meetings with your boss, your HR department and even your colleagues will send the message that you are motivated, open to communication and committed to doing things differently.

CHAPTER 6

Developing Your Political Strategy

"Do the best you can until you know better. Then when you know better, do better."

–Maya Angelou

The most important thing to remember is that getting politically savvy is neither an academic exercise nor a once-off episode. Rather, it is a skill that you should be developing over the course of your entire career. Like the woman I mentioned in Chapter 4, who made it a monthly practice to map her stakeholders and then spend the rest of that month managing them, developing your political strategy is something that you need to think about, implement and revisit on a regular basis. As you change and your context changes, so too should your strategy.

In this chapter, I will take you through several considerations for developing your political game plan. Marie McIntyre developed a decision tree that I have adapted by suggesting that you tackle a number of things simultaneously (rather than sequentially as she does). Building on my experience in strategy development and execution, I also include additional issues that I think you need to consider.

Start with the most important question of all

The very first thing that you need to establish is whether you are in danger of becoming The Problem. Or even worse, that you have already been tagged as The Problem.

I used to say in my workshops that it was unlikely that any of the delegates were considered The Problem by their company, since all of my lectures are for people who have been nominated by their company. I would then go on to joke: "Unless this is a last-ditch attempt to get you to change, of course…" Cue a loud round of laughter from everyone.

One day though, I had a delegate come up to me during the break and, with a stunned and pale face, say to me: "Actually, I think I *am* The Problem and that this *is* the last chance that the company is giving me." It was very sobering for her to realise quite how close to disaster she was getting and I could see from her reaction that she was suddenly understanding her situation very differently and was taking it extremely seriously.

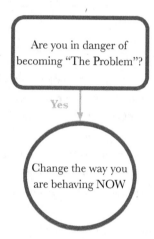

Figure 5: Priority #1 for any political strategy

If you think you are in the same situation, then before you do anything else, you need to take care of this. This assumes that it is not too late and quite frankly, it might be too late. It may well be that people have labelled you The Problem permanently and are only looking for – and finding – more and more evidence of what they have decided to be true.

There are many reasons why you might be The Problem. Maybe you are in a toxic environment where anything that resembles normal behaviour is seen as problematic? Perhaps you have been out of control emotionally, unable to get over things and you have shared your anger and frustration with anyone within earshot? Or possibly you have been looking for attention in all the wrong places, using up disproportionate amounts of your manager's energy and time? Whatever the reason, you need to start behaving differently immediately. Anything resembling whining must stop. Complaining and gossiping have got to come to an *immediate* end. Get yourself under control and then start to re-build how people see you, understanding that the longer you have been showing up in a problematic way, the more entrenched your brand is and the longer it is going to take for people to see you differently. If you want to keep your job though, you need to make every effort to persevere and to keep going, even when it feels like you're not getting anywhere.

If you are in a toxic environment though, it is unlikely that you are going to be able to change it. The risk you face is that just by acting 'normal' you are seen as The Problem. In this case, all my previous advice about toxic environments applies and you are going to need to think long and hard about how to get out of this environment with your confidence and sense of competence still intact.

Do you have any idea what it is you actually want?

Don Herold said something that I have always found particularly poignant:

"Unhappiness is not knowing what we want and killing ourselves to get it."

His observation has always made me think about what it is that drives me in the work that I do. Long ago, I realised that the problem I seek to solve, as a manager, a leader, a lecturer and a consultant, is the following:

On the one hand, Gallup's annual Global Employee Engagement Survey shows that – irrespective of company, industry or country – more and more employees are disengaged every year. In 2018, the number of employees who were "actively disengaged" or "not engaged" was 66% and while there was a lot of celebration in the fact that this was lower than many previous years, it is still, to my mind, an unacceptably high number of people who show up to work every day while being utterly switched off, mentally and emotionally.

On the other hand, numerous studies have shown that upwards of 80% of adults, when asked if they would want to continue to work if they were to become financially independent and so did not need to work, answer 'yes'.[81] In other words, we are wired as human beings to want to contribute and be part of something bigger than ourselves; to develop our talents and put them to good use. And yet most employees, the world over, are at work every day, just waiting for it to be over so that they can go home.

Of course, there can be many reasons for this. I have quite a few theories and see many of them play out in the consulting work that I do. I also wonder though if one of the reasons has to do with the fact that most people don't know what it is they want out of life or out of work. As such, to my mind getting clear on what you want to achieve is not just a critical step for your political strategy but for your life and how fulfilled (or not) you feel every day in what you wake up to do.

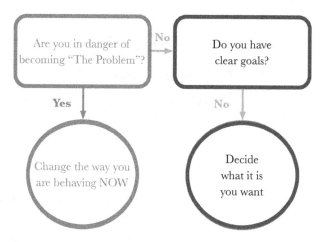

Figure 6: Setting goals

---

81   Kofman, 2006.

All of us have been at crossroads in our life when we are not sure what we want, or who we want to be. These inflection points are important times to stop, take a step back, get advice, reflect and recalibrate so we can move forward very clear on what we want to do and why. These can be planned inflection points, or completely impromptu, like when life throws something at us and our priorities suddenly become a lot clearer. That said, if you have *never* known what you want out of life and are just taking what comes as it comes, then I would suggest that you take some time to really think about what it is you want. If you are a corporate employee who has always wanted to be an entrepreneur, your political strategy to get you into your own business would be very different to an accountant who wants to be the head of a division within the next five years.

Some helpful advice to consider as you try to get clear on your goals is the following from Scott Anthony Barlow, the Founder and CEO of Happen to Your Career.

1. **Look behind you:**

    a. What do people always seem to come to you for?

    b. What are the things you love doing so much that you would do them for free?

    c. What do you do at work that's not part of your job and why do you do it?

2. **Look around you**

    a. How did you end up in your current
        i.   Profession,
        ii. Team,
        iii. Job and
        iv. Company?

    b. What do you love about where you are now?

    c. What would you change?

    d. What are the things that are non-negotiable for you in where you work, how you work and who you work with?

    Look at your answers to find patterns and think about to what degree you have been deliberate (or not) about what you want. Are you living your life or someone else's?

3. **Look ahead**

Start to apply what you know you love (and don't love) to where you want to go. Is it a particular role, profession or company? Is it something completely different?

Another concept that is powerful in helping us identify what it is we should or could be doing is the Japanese concept of "Ikigai", which means "reason for being". It takes four discrete elements and questions and looks at the intersection between them.

1. What you love doing
2. What you are good at
3. What you can be paid for
4. What the world needs

As the diagram opposite shows, your **passion** is the intersection point between what you love and what you are good at. Your **profession** combines what you are good at and what you can be paid for. Your **vocation** sits at the point where what you can be paid for and what the world needs come together. And finally, your **mission** is the overlap point between what you love and what the world needs.

Ikigai is when all four of these elements come together in your life. Even if three out of the four come together, something remains missing.

1. If you are doing what you love, what you are good at and what you can be paid for but are not doing something the world actually needs, you may be satisfied, but you will likely feel that you are really not making any positive difference in the world

2. Similarly, if you are doing what you love, what you are good at and what the world needs but you are not able to be paid for it, you may feel proud and fulfilled, but you don't earn anything. If you do not need to earn anything, there's obviously no problem but that's not a realistic option for most people.

3. The third possibility is that you are doing what you love, what the world needs and what you can be paid for, but you're not very good at it. While that's probably less likely than the other scenarios, it would

be a very tricky one to be in, because you are never sure when you are going to be caught out or come up against the limitations of your knowledge and skills.

4. The final possibility is that you are doing something that you are good at, that the world needs and that you can be paid for, but you don't love it. Alternatively, you used to love it but you don't love it anymore. While there is certainly comfort in knowing that you are unlikely to be unemployed, just 'going through the motions' with no sense of passion or commitment can also leave you feeling empty and that life has lost its flavour.

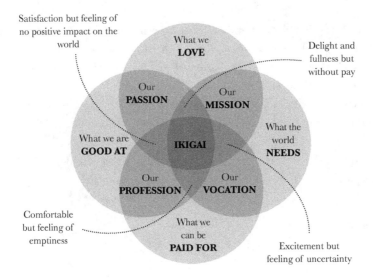

Figure 7: Ikigai Venn diagram

Crafting your strategy

Something I always find fascinating when I work with companies on their strategy is how many organisations equate goals with strategy. They are entirely different things. Goals are the 'what'. Strategy is the 'how'. And yet, most companies' strategies are just a re-framing of their goals. This is not just my experience, but something that lies at the heart of what Richard Rumelt, a true strategy guru, calls 'bad strategy.'

As he says, "good strategy almost always looks…simple and obvious and does not take a thick deck of PowerPoint slides to explain. It does not pop out of some "strategic management" tool, matrix, chart, triangle, or fill-in-the-blanks scheme. Instead, a talented leader identifies the one or two critical issues in the situation – the pivot points that can multiply the effectiveness of effort – and then focuses and concentrates action and resources on them. Despite the roar of voices wanting to equate strategy with ambition, leadership, "vision," planning, or the economic logic of competition, strategy is none of these. The core of strategy work is always the same: discovering the critical factors in a situation and designing a way of coordinating and focusing actions to deal with those factors."[82]

The same principles apply when you are developing your personal political strategy. What are the critical things that you need to get right and what are you going to *do* to make that possible? "A good strategy includes a set of coherent actions. They are not "implementation" details; they are the punch in the strategy. A strategy that fails to define a variety of plausible and feasible immediate actions is missing a critical component."

In my experience, there are four things you need to consider as building blocks in your strategy and most importantly, do something about.

---

82   Rumelt, 2011.

Figure 8: Political strategy questions to change a situation

Are you using your energy well?

If the answer is "no", what are you going to do about it? In Chapter 2 I spoke about economics as being about the study of the allocation of finite resources in the face of infinite demands. What is true of economics is as true of our energy. We all have a limited amount of energy with which to tackle every day and an unending list of demands on that energy. How you conserve, build and use your energy matters if you want to show up in the best possible way, achieve what you are trying to and stay resilient in the face of setbacks and obstacles.

One of the best books on the benefits of focussing energy is Greg McKeown's wonderful *Essentialism: The Disciplined Pursuit of Less*. He poses questions of the reader that I think we can all relate to: "Have you ever felt both overworked *and* underutilised? Have you ever found yourself majoring in minor activities? Do you ever feel busy but not productive?"[83]

His way of getting out of this trap, one where we feel we are making "a millimetre of progress in a million directions" is to give focussed attention and energy to the few things that matter the most. He stresses that this isn't about "setting New Year's resolutions to say 'no' more, or about pruning your in-box, or about mastering some new strategy in time management. It is about constantly pausing to ask "Am I investing in the right activities?" There are far more activities and opportunities in the world than we have time and resources to invest in. And although many of them may be good, or even very good, the fact is that most are trivial and very few are vital."

Which then begs us all to ask the question, "What is vital for me?" and to realise the truth in his point:

"If you don't prioritise your life, someone else will."

Most of us know what gives us energy and what drains it. The 'knowing' is therefore not the challenge. Rather, we fail in the 'doing'. Sometimes the doing comes down to absolute basics. In an assignment that I set after a lecture, I asked delegates to develop their own political game plan and one of the managers in the group came back with the insight that she has higher energy levels in the morning than the afternoon and so she needed to structure her time accordingly. Knowing that she did well in meetings in the morning but better on detailed, deep work in the afternoon, she set about scheduling her diary differently. In this way, she maximised her energy, contribution and wellbeing; not to mention her ability to end a day feeling that she had achieved what she actually needed to.

---

83   McKeown, 2014

Do you have opposition?

This can be a difficult one to face up to, not least because it often centres on questions of ego and identity. In another assignment I set, a student put it in a way that I think most of us can relate to. "Managing my adversaries must have been the toughest part for me, firstly to acknowledge and then to action. The very dominant and slightly stubborn part of me has up until this point felt comfortable with colleagues that I do not interact well with. I feel that they are luckily not in control of my career and therefore, I will not spend even a minute reflecting on their point of view. It was with the concept of a "Chief Whisperer" however, that cold water ran over me when I realised that my biggest adversary is the number one whisperer."

She explained that she and the "Chief Whisperer" had had a falling out and things had never really improved since then. She then went on to point out that the whisperer was a "personal friend of my manager and although I was aware of this, it was not a concern as the relationship that I have with my line manager is very good. It was, however, when reflecting on the influence that such a whisperer can have on my career that I realised that I am the losing party." Wisely, she concluded that she needed to build bridges and not take the risk of jeopardising the way that her manager saw her – even at a subconscious level. She then turned this realisation into action.

In the same way, you need to think about who stands between you and what you want to achieve and why they might be blocking you. You can do this by drawing on all the things that I have highlighted so far:

- If you dislike them, have you allowed your feelings of dislike to get in the way of getting on with the things that you need to achieve professionally?

- Have you put yourself in their shoes and tried to understand what matters to them?

- Have you thought about what conditions they might have for supporting you and being converted to an ally?

- Are you prepared, willing and able to meet those conditions?

- If not, how can you minimise the fallout from the fact that they are an adversary?

Do you have enough (of the right) support?

Support is one thing. The *right* support is another. Do you have enough support from people in positions of power and influence relative to what you are trying to get done? It doesn't have to be people who are senior to you. Of course, it often is, but support and influence comes in all kinds of packages and sits at all levels in a team, department and organisation.

Think of whose support you need to achieve your goals. They might be managers, they may be colleagues, and they may be people in an entirely different part of the organisation or even a different organisation entirely.

- Do they know you and do you know them?

- If not, how can you get them into your network?

- What would be the best way of letting them know what you want to achieve? Directly telling someone certainly works, but often you need to be a bit more circumspect and subtle.

- How can you get them to advocate for you? What can you offer them in return so that it is a mutually beneficial relationship rather than just a one-way street?

Do you have enough leverage?

As we discussed in Chapter 4, there are all manner of things that give you leverage – skills, reputation, contacts, seniority, etc.

- Which of these do you have and how much leverage do they give you at the moment?

- Are you using the leverage you have, to your advantage?

- If you don't have a lot of leverage, how might you get more?

  o Do you need to add to your skills (by additional studying for example)?

o   Do you need to build your experience (for example, by volunteering for a new assignment that would stretch you)?

• Are you seen as critical to your team or organisation, or are you considered dispensable by those who matter? If you are considered dispensable, or even worse, not considered at all because you are invisible to those who matter, what are you going to do to fix it?

Maintaining your political strategy

If none of the issues I've highlighted above feature in your current situation, then you would seem to be in a good political position.

However, there are, as always, two caveats:

1. You may have missed something, so don't get too complacent, too quickly.

2. Things are always changing. You need to be alert to changes so you can adjust your plan as the context shifts.

That said, even if your assessment is spot on and you *are* doing well politically, you still need to have a strategy for maintaining your political capital. This may require a combination of things that you will stop and start, as well as activities and behaviours that you will continue doing.

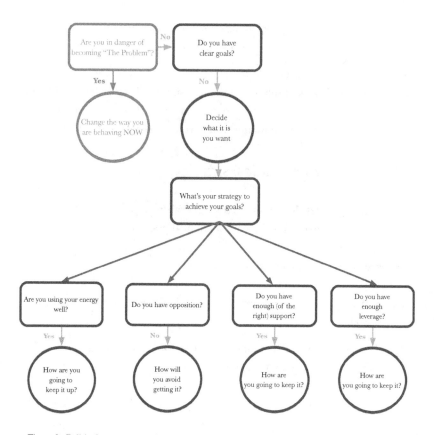

Figure 9: Political strategy questions to maintain a situation

- If you *are* using your energy well, congratulations! Now how are you going to ensure that it doesn't slip and that you don't get into habits that don't serve you?

- If you *don't* have opposition, give yourself a pat on the back. What do you need to continue to do to make sure it stays that way?

- If you *do* have enough of the right support, again, take a bow. What are you going to do to keep that support and ideally build it?

- If you *do* have enough leverage, again, how are you going to *keep* it? How are you going to remain relevant and current and ensure that you and your skills continue to be seen as indispensable?

Closing Thoughts

I wrote the bulk of this book during the COVID-19 lockdown in South Africa and am typing these final thoughts on Day 85 of a shutdown that has seen things change dramatically in workplaces and economies the world over, and the seasons change from summer to autumn. It has been a harrowing time for many, a time of reinvention and opportunity for others, and a time of uncertainty for everyone.

The question I heard asked at the beginning of lockdown was whether we were going through a storm, a winter or an Ice Age. While I am leaning towards an Ice Age, it is a question I am still unable to answer as we all try to hazard guesses and marshall our hopes. Will everything that has happened – and is happening still – herald an entirely new way of working? One that sees offices around the world empty out dramatically as people and organisations redefine what is possible in terms of how, where and when we work and live rich and productive lives that are not defined by cubicles and timesheets? Or will we slowly, cautiously and gingerly go back to the (pre)familiar, picking up the work lives and routines that we always knew and in so doing, pick up the old habits, expectations, irritations, frustrations, metrics and connections that defined them?

Recently, I was a speaker on a webinar and the question asked was whether remote working eliminates office politics. By definition, if no-one is in an office, surely office politics are impossible? I made the point that in fact, entirely the opposite is true. Remote working makes the relationships, perceptions, connections and informal influence that lie at the heart of office politics, even *more* critical than they already are.

Again, this may come as good news to some and bad news to others. Many people, when making the move to working remotely, can't wait for all the upsides – no longer having to commute, no longer having to deal with unnecessary interruptions and distractions and best of all, no politics! What research shows though, is that remote working has all manner of challenges and that the social and political challenges that people face when working 'in real life' (IRL) are in fact amplified when working virtually.

The research that existed prior to COVID-19 is clearly based on situations where there was a combination of people in an office working together and others who worked remotely. Such situations certainly have several differences to a situation where the majority, if not all, of a team are working remotely. Nonetheless, there are still findings that are worth bearing in mind from the research that has been done on the topic. This includes that people report feeling excluded and out of the loop to a far greater degree when they are working remotely than when they work together IRL. Studies have found that conflict tends to escalate a lot more quickly when people are not physically working together, and that it takes a lot longer to resolve. Added to all of this is the (valid) concern expressed by people working remotely that they are considered less hard working and less committed to their careers than colleagues who arrive at the office every day.

The constant advice given to people working virtually therefore, is to not focus on 'the task' at the expense of 'the relationships' – exactly the same advice I give throughout this book. In the discussion that followed the presentations, advice from me and another speaker and me was confirmed repeatedly. As human beings, we are social creatures and that doesn't go away simply by virtue of not being physically present with our colleagues. We crave connection, we crave inclusion, we crave belonging and we crave meaning. Becoming skilled and smart at office politics and playing them ethically, is the best way to achieve all of those cravings, at work.

I wish you luck navigating your career and in using what I have shared in this book, to take you, your team and your organisation to greater heights.

References

Bauer, T. & Erdogan, B. 2010. *Organizational Behavior.* Version 1.1. Irvington, NY: Flat World Knowledge.

Bolman, L.G. & Deal, T.E. 1997. *Reframing Organizations: Artistry, choice and leadership.* 2nd Edition. San Francisco: Jossey-Bass Publishers.

Braddy, P. & Campbell, M. 2014. *Using Political Skill to Maximize and Leverage Work Relationships.* [Online] Available at: https://www.ccl.org/wp-content/uploads/2015/04/UsingPoliticalSkill.pdf [Accessed 18 February 2020].

Chappelow, C. & Leslie, J. n.d. *Throwing the Right Switches: How to keep your Executive Career on Trac.* [Online] Available at: https://www.ccl.org/articles/white-papers/throwing-the-right-switches-how-to-keep-your-executive-career-on-track/ [Accessed March 16 2020].

Chen, J. 2019. *Anchoring.* Retrieved from: https://www.investopedia.com/terms/a/anchoring.asp [Accessed 12 April 2020].

Covey, S. 2004. *The 7 Habits of Highly Effective People.* 2nd ed. New York: Free Press.

Davis, J. 2016. *The Greats on Leadership.* London: Nicholas Brealey Publishing.

Ferris, G.R. Treadway, D.C., Kolodinsky, R. & Hochwarter, W. 2005. Development and validation of the political skill inventory. *Journal of Management 31,* 126-152.

Feuerman, M. 2017. *The Gottman Institute.* [Online] Available at: https://www.gottman.com/blog/managing-vs-resolving-conflict-relationships-blueprints-success/ [Accessed 19 March 2020].

Jarrett, M. 2017. *The 4 Types of Organizational Politics.* [Online] Available at: https://hbr.org/2017/04/the-4-types-of-organizational-politics [Accessed 20 February 2020].

Kaiser, R.B., Chamorro-Premuzic, T. & Lusk, D. 2017. *Harvard Business Review.* [Online] Available at: https://hbr.org/2017/09/playing-office-politics-without-selling-your-soul?referral=03759&cm_vc=rr_item_page.bottom [Accessed 22 March 2020].

Kofman, F. 2006. *Conscious Business: How to build value through values.* Boulder, CO: Sounds True.

Krawcheck, S. 2016. *The Single Biggest Mistake I've Seen Women Make at Work.* [Online] Available at: https://www.linkedin.com/pulse/single-biggest-mistake-ive-seen-women-make-work-sallie-krawcheck/ [Accessed 2 February 2020].

Lencioni, P. 2005. *Overcoming the Five Dysfunctions of a Team – A Field Guide.* San Francisco: Jossey-Bass.

McIntyre, M. G. 2005. *Secrets to Winning at Office Politics.* New York: St. Martins Griffin.

McKee, A. 2015. *Harvard Business Review.* [Online] Available at: https://hbr.org/2015/01/office-politics-is-just-influence-by-another-name [Accessed 5 April 2020].

McKeown, G. 2014. *Essentialism: The Disciplined Pursuit of Less.* United Kingdom: Virgin Books.

Mindtools. 2019. *Mindtools.* [Online] Available at: https://www.mindtools.com/community/pages/article/newLDR_56.php [Accessed 5 April 2020].

Ngozi Adichie, C. 2009. *The danger of a single story.* Retrieved from: https://www.ted.com/talks/chimamanda_ngozi_adichie_the_danger_of_a_single_story [Accessed 12 April 2020].

Peters, T. 1997. *The Brand Called You.* [Online] Available at: https://www.fastcompany.com/28905/brand-called-you [Accessed 10 April 2020].

Player, A., de Moura, G.R., Leite, A.C., Abrams, D. & Tresh, F. 2019. *Overlooked Leadership Potential: The Preference for Leadership Potential in Job Candidates Who Are Men vs. Women.* [Online] Available at: https://www.frontiersin.org/articles/10.3389/fpsyg.2019.00755/full [Accessed 1 April 2020].

Reardon, K.K. 2015. Managing Internal Politics. In: *Business Essential.* London: Bloomsbury Publishing, pp. 58 - 61.

Rumelt, R. 2011. *Good Strategy/Bad Strategy: The difference and why it matters.* London: Profile Books.

Sandberg, S. 2013. *Lean In.* New York: Random House.

Scott, E. 2020. *How to Apologize More Sincerely.* [Online] Available at: https://www.verywellmind.com/how-to-apologize-more-sincerely-3144467 [Accessed 10 April 2020].

Spicer, A. 2014. *Cass Business School.* [Online] Available at: https://www.cass.city.ac.uk/faculties-and-research/research/cass-knowledge/2014/june/acquiring-political-intelligence [Accessed 20 March 2020].

Todd, S., Harris, K.S. & Harris, R.B. 2009. Career Success Implications of Political Skill. *The Journal of Social Psychology,* 149(3), pp. 279 - 304.

Wasserman, H. 2019. *The SA minibus taxi industry is absolutely massive – here's everything you need to know.* Retrieved from: https://www.businessinsider.co.za/how-big-is-south-african-taxi-industry-2019-5 [Accessed 12 April 2020].

Wenderoth, M. C. 2016. *Great Leaders Embrace Office Politics.* [Online] Available at: https://hbr.org/2016/04/great-leaders-embrace-office-politics [Accessed 11 April 2020].

Index

CPSIA information can be obtained
at www.ICGtesting.com
Printed in the USA
LVHW081748101220
673847LV00015B/1888